HOW TO
BETT
DIORAMAS

CW00740094

BARRY FORD

Series editor: Michael G. Reccia
Series production: David Openshaw

Published by: Happy Medium Press (www.scififantasymodeller.co.uk)
Copyright © Happy Medium Press 2010

ISBN: 978-0-9564306-0-1

Printed in Great Britain by the MPG Books Group, Bodmin and King's Lynn

CONTENTS

5: Introduction

From the Ground Up

An introduction

W e live in interesting times. Actually, I was going to begin this introduction by saying 'It was the best of times, it was the worst of times', but apparently somebody beat me to it. On reflection, 'We live in interesting times' is probably more appropriate as we *do* live in interesting times – as a society as a whole and also as model makers.

Over the last few years we have seen the decline of the high street model shop, and those few that survive have had to evolve in order to do so, by today also having to stock such things as 'collectables' and toys. This is a symptom of the way we now shop as a society as a whole, and of a declining interest in the hobby: whilst dyed in the wool model makers have far from lost their enthusiasm, there does not appear to be a great amount of young blood to take up the mantel as the current generation of modellers grows older.

Things are far from all doom and gloom, however, as, whilst the hobby is losing its mass-market appeal, the advent of the Internet has allowed us model makers to enjoy a greater sense of

community than ever before; those models that *are* being produced are more readily available from any corner of the globe, and they tend to be of better quality as they are made by enthusiasts for enthusiasts. In short, the times they are a-changing. Don't tell me... that's another line someone has beaten me to.

During the course of this book I intend to discuss the various techniques I have learned, used and developed over thirty-five years of model making, with a particular emphasis on the building and painting of dioramas, vignettes and figures. Whilst I still find it fun to take kit parts out of a box and build a stand-alone model, over the years I have come to enjoy building dioramas more, as, not only do I get to stretch my model making skills in new and different directions, but I find it very satisfying to be able to create a scene and tell a story in three dimensions. I have attempted to look at modelling techniques that are relevant to different scales for each chapter of this book and to try to cover a different environment for each scale.

Whilst I will be discussing specific techniques within each chapter, this is not a book for the novice modeller, as I will not be going into basic skills such as how to glue parts together, or simple paint or decal application. The aim of discussing the techniques I have used to make the models in this book is not so much to create a 'how-to' guide as to hopefully inspire you to interpret some of my ideas when creating your own models. Please note that each project in this book has been made over a three to four week period, whilst also trying to fit in those daft little things like eating, sleeping and holding down a full time job. Whilst I am sure that the dioramas could have been developed further given more time, hopefully each project will act as a 'starter for ten' to demonstrate what can be achieved within a limited period.

Before going any further I would like to touch on three concepts I believe are vital to the evolution of our model making skills.

Observation

In order to make our models look more realistic we have to appreciate what something looks like

in real life, even when modelling fantastic subjects for which there are no real life equivalents. For example, consider weathering a model such as the *Mole* from **Thunderbirds**... I am sure this will come as a shock to you, as it did to me, but *the Mole does not actually exist.* What *do* exist, however, are tanks and construction vehicles that share many of the same design features. By observing these vehicles we can understand how the passage of time and the demands of environment affect them and then apply that knowledge to our science fiction and

fantasy subjects. Similarly, when creating a diorama, whether it is set in a built or a natural environment, we can apply our knowledge of what we see around us as we go about our daily business to create a more realistic scene.

Holistic Modelling

It is a natural human trait to want to learn about the things we are interested in and I am sure that you, like me, read modelling magazines and books that cover the subjects that are the focus of your model making skills. So, science fiction and fantasy modellers will probably read *Science Fiction and Fantasy Modeller*, *Amazing Figure Modeler*, *Kitbuilders* and the like. Similarly, tank builders will read *AFV*, train enthusiasts will read *Model Railroader*, etc. It seems to me that, whilst we all build subjects from different genres, a lot of techniques are interchangeable between subjects, and so, by embracing techniques from other genres of model making, we can improve our skills when applying them to our own specific genre. Examples? – Learning weathering from tank builders or landscape building from railway modellers. This holistic approach can not only be applied to techniques but also to materials: a model railway tree can become a bush in your 1:12 scale diorama, or a 1:24 scale car driver can look just as at home at the wheel of a time-travelling *DeLorean* as he can in a rally car.

Experimentation

Do not be afraid to try new techniques or subjects when modelling. Whatever the outcome you will have learned something that you can add to that modelling database in your head. If the new technique works – *great*, as you can then go on to apply that knowledge to future projects. If it doesn't work consider why it was unsuccessful and either don't try that again, or work out what went wrong so that it doesn't happen when you *do* try it again. Also, don't be afraid of moving on from a model you are not happy with; it does you no good to press on with something you have lost your enthusiasm for, and you can always return to it in time with a fresh pair of eyes that will enable you to complete it to your satisfaction.

Just before you get comfy and settle down on the sofa, bed or toilet to read this book (and I trust you are sitting comfortably rather than trying to read this book in the shop without buying it) I think I should just touch on my own model making philosophy. I think I would best describe myself as an Impressionistic Model Maker, which perhaps needs a little elaboration. Whilst working on a model I always try to bear in mind that, whilst the subject is being held six inches or so from my face, it will generally be viewed from a distance of two to three feet away. This means that I only create or paint what will be seen at this general viewing distance. To put it in the vernacular: I am not a rivet counter. Whilst that may sound a little glib you have to remember that, if you are looking at a 1:48 scale

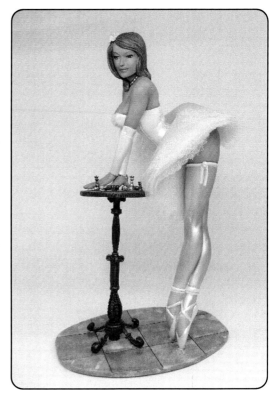

model from a couple of feet away, that's the equivalent of viewing the full size subject from 48 times further away, meaning you wouldn't be able to make out every hair on Jessica Alba's head but you would be able to see that she had a nice hair-do – that's if you were looking at her hair. On a similar basis I am more concerned that, when you look at one of my completed models, it conveys the essence of what it is meant to be to you than I am about whether the third panel from the left on the *Starship Enterprise* should be 3.6mm long or 3.8mm long. I also take a similar attitude towards colour: after many years of studying film stills, reading magazine articles, watching videos and attending exhibitions to try and work out the correct colour of a subject I have come to the conclusion that *there is no such thing as the correct colour*. Please don't get me wrong: I am not suggesting that you paint *Thunderbird 2* orange (but if you want to – why not – it's your model), but you do come to realise that the

colour of a subject depends upon the light under which it is viewed, the type of film stock used to photograph the subject, the definition of the monitor you are using and how it is set and the paper and ink quality used for publication – and that's before you even take into account different filming models for different scenes and repairs carried out to studio models during the course of filming. In a very long-winded way all I am trying to say is that it's your model and, as long as you are happy with it, that's all that matters. Life is too short not to enjoy what you are doing as a hobby.

On a final note I would like to thank Mike and Dave from *Happy Medium Press* for having enough faith in me to want to publish this book and Des from the *Manchester Modelzone* for getting us together in the first place. Most importantly of all, I would like to dedicate this book to my Mum and Dad: June and Fred Ford, without whom I would not be here. Apart from the obvious biological reason, it is only down to their faith in me, and their moral and practical encouragement, that I am able to do what I can and be the person that I am. My Dad died in 1986 and my Mum, who has always been my rock and the wind beneath my wings, passed away in 2008.

Barry Ford 2010

Classic Confrontation

Constructing a 1/35th scale Batmobile

and figure diorama

Let me begin by saying that Military modellers are jammy so-and-sos. I know they have their rivets to count, but that is a small cross to bear when you consider how well they are serviced by the model making industry. For a start they have an extremely wide range of commercially released kits of Armoured Fighting Vehicles and Figures, that are generally very well made, readily available and to a consistent 1:35 scale. Secondly, these releases are supplemented by numerous aftermarket parts and conversion kits to make the models even more detailed. And, as if that wasn't enough, there is an entire industry producing in-scale accessories to enable the model maker to create dioramas, along with a plethora of model buildings and landscape architecture.

Meanwhile, the Science Fiction and Fantasy modeller, up until recently, has had to put up with a small selection of film– and television– related subjects, the dimensions of which manufacturers seem to arrive at by asking 'will the parts fit in the box available' rather than 'is the subject to a recognised scale?' Well, we Science Fiction and Fantasy modellers are revolting – the author in particular, some might say. Over recent years we have been fortunate enough to see limited run kits being produced to consistent scales and a burgeoning aftermarket parts industry.

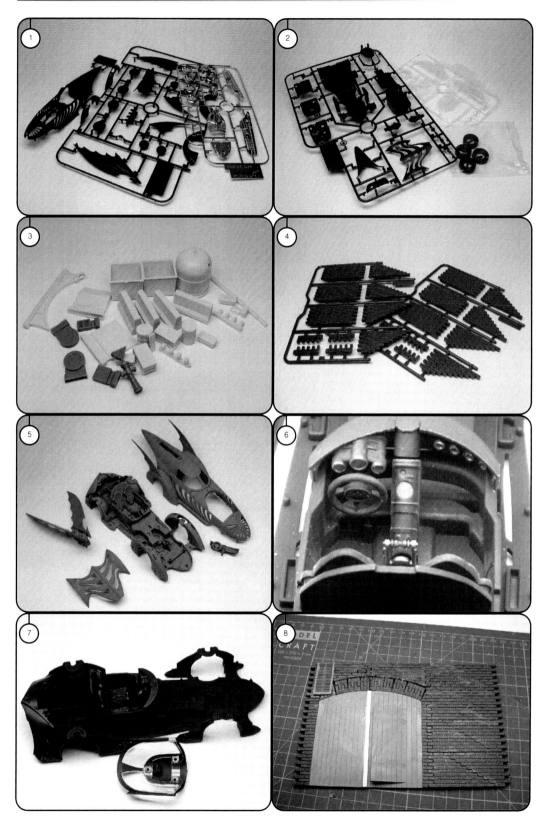

1-2: *Batmobile* kit parts. 3: *Resin City*
accessories. 4: *Tamiya* wall sections.
5: *Batmobile* sub-assemblies primed.
6: *Batmobile* interior completed with drybrush
weathering and gloss varnish to dials.
7: interior fitted to body and windscreen fitted to
canopy following painting of exterior.
8: wall section assembled on a flat surface to
ensure rigidity whilst glue sets.
9-10: *Batmobile* lighting tested prior to final
assembly. Inset: completed *Batmobile*.

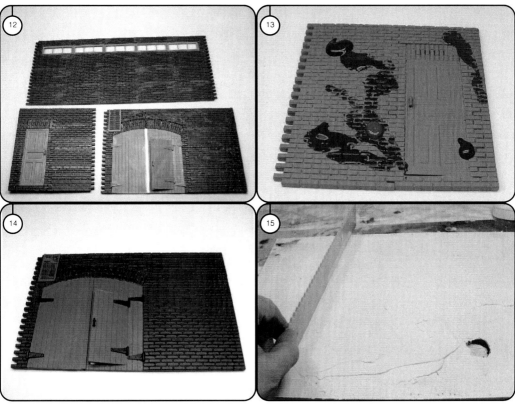

But, as the old adage goes: if you can't beat them – join them. Does this mean I'm going to give up *Batmobiles* for tanks? No, but it does seem daft not to take advantage of the material that is out there.

Over the last few years Japanese manufacturer *Bandai* has released a set of three highly detailed *Batmobile* kits based on the vehicles from the popular feature films. These include the bullet-nosed car from the Tim Burton directed films; the ornate vehicle from **Batman Forever** and the 'I gotta get one of those' *Tumbler* from the recent films starring Christian Bale.

At first it seemed strange that *Bandai* should release these kits in 1:35 scale rather than the traditional 1:24 scale that is often used for car kits. But, when you consider that some of these are more like Armoured Fighting Vehicles than something you would nip to *Tesco's* in on a Saturday morning, you begin to see the logic. The other advantage, of course, is that it enables you to enhance them by using some of the diorama kits that are available.

For this particular diorama I decided to use the **Batman Forever** *Batmobile*, partly because I was intrigued as to how such a small model could be effectively lit, as advertised, but also because, with its wildly exaggerated bat wings, it had a slightly more 'comic-book' appearance that would tie in nicely with the *Batman* figure I was intending to use. In terms of design, this *Batmobile* is a

11: trial layout of diorama with basic components and models. 12: individual wall panels assembled prior to painting.

13: wall panel primed. Paint applied directly to wall before mixing in situ. 14: base colours for wall panel complete prior to final

weathering and application of mortar. 15: *Resin Stucco* applied to base and levelled with a straight edge. 16: the completed

wall sections.

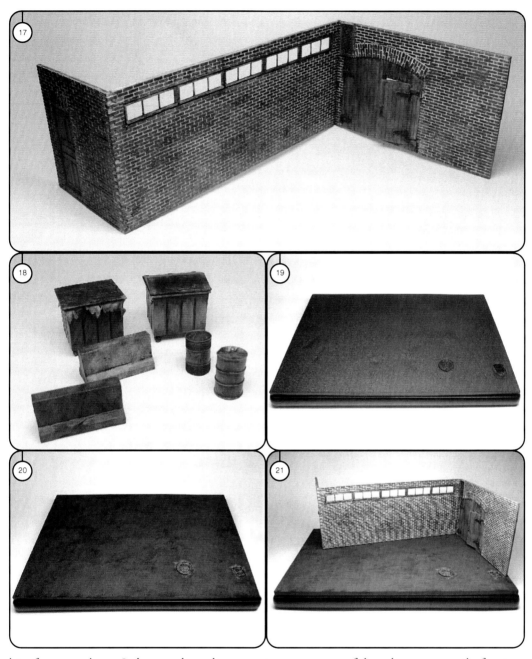

bit of a strange beast. It does not have the aggressive appearance of the other cars to strike fear into the criminal fraternity, and does seem strangely vulnerable to attack with that open framework exposing the engine. However, it is still of an interesting design that I felt would work well with the diorama I had planned.

I bought the *Batman* figure in the late eighties and it came in a twin pack with *The Joker*, cast in white metal, for use with *Mayfair Games'* Role Playing Game based on the *DC* Superheroes. Whilst several sets of white metal figures were produced for the game, the majority of them were

17: wall panels assembled in final arrangement. 18: street furniture painted and weathered. 19: base colours applied to tarmac and manhole cover. 20: sponge applied final colour to tarmac. 21: wall panels arranged and glued to base. 22: stained tissue paper and other detritus added to base. 23: close-up of leaves in gutter and moss on walls. 24: close-up of completed 'garage' doors and leaves piled up against walls.

in the traditional 25mm scale used for this kind of figure. This set, however, was produced at the larger 1:35 scale and the figures appear to be based on Brian Bolland's rendition of the characters in *The Killing Joke* graphic novel.

To create a scene for the characters I purchased four sets of *Tamiya's* 1:35 *Brick Walls*. These comprise of two sprues of brickwork panels that have toothed ends to allow for accurate bonding between the pieces. On the down side the panels are quite small, so you will need quite a few to construct part of a building. On the positive side they are fairly cheap at around £3 per packet. To add to the building details I bought a couple of boxes of *MiniArts' House Accessories* sets, which include four sprues containing various doors, windows and guttering. To complete the scene I added *Mig's* resin *Modern City Accessories* and *Plus Model's* manhole covers and gullys to my purchases.

I started off by building the *Batmobile* so that I would have a better idea as to the size of the completed diorama that would fit around it. Whilst the instructions are completely in Japanese

the diagrams were clear enough to follow easily. I started by gluing the parts together, then quickly realised that this was intended to be a snap-together kit. I think most of us have our preconceptions of what a snap kit is like as we have all probably come across loose fitting parts that really need to be glued together to get a satisfactory finish. Not on this kit, though, as the parts fit was very tight and the join between parts would have been admired on a more traditional glue-together kit. A word of caution, though: the parts fit is so tight that any pre-painted parts need to be scraped clean before joining to ensure that the parts don't jam together half way down the connecting lugs – trust me, I can confirm this from bitter experience.

For the construction of the *Batmobile* I generally followed the instructions provided, but sub-divided them into sub-assemblies for ease of painting. I also built the light and battery box first to ensure that it was working correctly before I fitted it inside the model.

The overall colour of the car is obviously black – but what type of black to use? Looking at reference photographs and the film itself the vehicle does have a sheen to it, but not the obvious sheen of a gloss finish, and even a satin finish seemed to be too reflective. On the other hand, a true matt finish would seem too dull. I therefore decided to use a black from the *Liquitex Artist's Acrylics* range, which tend to dry with a very slight sheen that sometimes needs to be dulled down with a coat of matt varnish for most models. There are two types of black available: Ivory Black and Mars Black. As I'm sure you appreciate, most blacks are actually incredibly dark shades of grey or brown. Ivory Black is a red-based black, but Mars Black is a blue-based black that is ideal for this model.

I airbrushed all external parts in Mars Black, but painted the inside and the underside of the car *Vallejo* Matt Black to give a slight variation in the paint scheme. Some details on the underside were picked up with *Games Workshop* Boltgun Metal along with some drybrushing with the same colour and some Raw Sienna.

For the car interior I gave the Matt Black a drybrushing with Raw Sienna to simulate a little wear and painted the dials blue with a silver trim. Once dry I filled the dial recesses with gloss varnish.

The outer rims of the hubcaps were painted Boltgun Metal, although the inside was left chrome-plated. Whilst the centre of the hub caps come with the bat symbol engraved on them I decided to be lazy and, rather than paint the symbols, I applied the supplied self-adhesive decals. The rear of the wheels were painted Boltgun Metal and then weathered by wiping on and off *Liquitex Charcoal Acrylic Woodstain*. The tyres were weathered by drybrushing an Earth colour. The rear exhausts, whilst metallic in finish on the real thing, are not as bright as the supplied chrome plastic parts, so I airbrushed *Vallejo* Metallic Black over these parts to tone them down. The chrome exposed engine parts were treated to a wipe on/wipe off of *Charcoal Woodstain* to give them a little weathering and the painting of the sub-assemblies was completed.

25-26: weathering/dirtying-down is achieved by adding dust to the street scene.

27

Base flesh and grey colours added to primed figure.

28

Flesh and grey shading added using washes.

29

Grey areas highlighted with a combination of drybrushing and blending of colours.

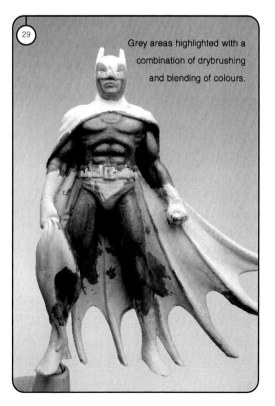

30

Base coat of blue.

Blue shading added by blending darker shades to base colour.

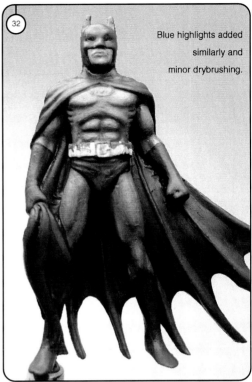

Blue highlights added similarly and minor drybrushing.

Completed 1/35th scale *Batman*...

...and *Batman*'s cape.

35: initial paint scheme on *The Joker* – colours added from the flesh to outer layers of clothing.

36: the Joker completed using similar techniques to *Batman* figure. 37: *The Joker* placed in the final diorama.

With initial painting complete I constructed the *Batmobile* following the kit's instructions and, as noted earlier, was most impressed with the parts fit for a snap fit kit. When the model was completed I installed the light and battery box and lit the car up and was very pleased with the results from such a small LED. To pose the car I rotated the wheels to show off their unique axle arrangements and decided to leave the canopy open. I also decided to have the tail fins parted as it emphasised the slightly 'camp' design of the car, and this was the one part of the kit that did not want to stay shut without glue. The inside of the tail fin was painted Metallic Black for further variation in tones and all that was needed to complete the car was to carry out a little weathering by drybrushing Neutral Grey, Raw Sienna and Earth Brown.

With the *Batmobile* complete I turned my attention to the building work. I had no intention of creating a full height building and decided that walls four brick panels high would be more than sufficient for the diorama.

I started off by building a short section of wall containing a pair of large wooden doors with an arched head and included pass-gate. Whilst in an ideal world I would have kept the brickwork and doors and windows separate until painting was complete, the construction of the wall sections required the inclusion of the doors and windows at this stage to help hold everything in one piece. The one disadvantage of the *Tamiya* brick panels is that they do need to be cut around unusual shapes with a small saw, as they are too thick to score with a knife. As the head of the door was arched I chose to include some soldier course brickwork as a lintel and this involved cutting very small sections of brickwork and gluing them to the door head. The curvature of the arch was marked on a brick panel and I heavily scored the line with a strong knife blade. It would have been impossible to cut out these curved sections with the saw I had used for the other panels and would have taken an age to score out with the hobby knife. Fortunately I have in my modelling arsenal a very small saw from *Tamiya* that is ideal for getting into awkward places, and it also comes with a blade that is reasonably flexible. With the groove scored into the brickwork panel I slid the flexible saw blade into it and was able to remove the unwanted section quite quickly. The doors were completed with the addition of hinges and handles.

I decided that the main wall behind the *Batmobile* should be fairly plain, as it would be mostly hidden behind the car, so I created a section of brickwork five panels wide by three panels tall. To break the wall up I added a ribbon of long, narrow windows and cut out further brickwork panels to get the wall to the same height as the adjacent section. I did not include any feature brickwork for the lintel above these windows as I justified that the brickwork above them would be supported by a hidden steel lintel. See, I can bore you just as much with construction technology as I can with model making. I created a third wall panel to give the scene further depth and incorporated a standard door with feature brickwork over, not only to break up the bare bricks, but also because I was rapidly running out of brick panels and didn't fancy a trip to the model shop on a cold February morning. Prior to giving the completed brick panels a coat of grey primer I used two-part epoxy putty to fill in the odd gaps between bricks – particularly to the over door arch, blending the putty in to look like over-large mortar joints.

38-39: two views of the completed street scene.

There are many ways to paint brickwork, and this is just one of them. If you observe real brickwork you will notice that there is a variation in colour in any given brick wall, which stems from three main factors. Bricks are generally made from clay and are fired in a kiln – as you will appreciate, depending on where any particular brick is in the oven it will receive slightly different levels of heat than the other bricks and so you will find some bricks which are 'under-done' and others with 'crispy bits', which all goes to create the colour variation. Also, bricks have different textures, which will not only reflect light in different ways, but also dictate the amount of weathering that will affect the brick. Which leads me on to my third point: that even with a smooth brick that has a fairly consistent colouring, such as an 'Accrington Red', weathering will affect the brick colouring dependent on its orientation and general environment.

As an aside, whenever I come across *Accrington Brick* I am reminded of the time when, as a junior technician, I went out to the *Accrington Brick Quarry* to survey it. My colleague was taking readings using a theodolite and I was holding the levelling staff. As I stood in one particular position to allow my colleague to take a reading I realised that I was slowly sinking into the ground. I shouted for help across the quarry, but my colleague was so busy taking readings that he did not hear me until he lifted his head and yelled to me to stop moving the staff about. By this time mud was seeping over the top of my boots and my colleague had to fetch a spade from his car to dig me out.

I have come across suggestions that one way of painting brickwork is to apply a base colour and then pick out odd bricks, in a random pattern, to give a variation in colour. Whilst this is a valid method it does imply that each brick is a consistent colour in and of itself. However, when closely observed, each brick will have colour variations across it. To replicate this effect I apply and mix paint colours directly onto the brickwork, making sure the colours are not too well mixed – thereby resulting in the necessary variations. Brickwork comes in many colours so I elected to go for a red-brown tone by using *Liquitex* Red Oxide and Raw Umber, with the odd spot of green. To add further variation I drybrushed the face of the brickwork with a lighter shade of the Red Oxide.

With the bricks painted I turned my attention to the mortar, and, as with brickwork, there are a large variety of colours to choose from, although the colouring will be a little more consistent across its length. Rather than going for a mortar to blend in with the brickwork I went for a contrasting colour and used *Liquitex Almond Woodstain*. This was liberally applied over the face of the brickwork and quickly wiped off before it had dried. The *Woodstain* has a low viscosity and stays in the mortar joints as it is wiped off the face of the bricks. Any stubborn areas can be removed with a slightly moist cloth. To add some further variation in colour across the whole wall I dabbed on some *Charcoal Woodstain* and again wiped it off before it could dry.

The doors and windows were painted green. The paint was not applied carefully as any minor splashes onto the brickwork could well have happened in real life and I wanted the woodwork to look as if it had not been particularly well cared for. To further distress the wood I applied *White*

and *Charcoal* woodstains as described earlier. The wall panels were then sprayed with a matt varnish before assembling them into the desired layout.

It was at this stage that I loosely arranged the parts on the baseboard to get a feel for the final composition and to review which of the scale accessories to use. The recycling bin was too large to incorporate within the scene and the additional concrete barriers and crates did not fit, in both senses of the word. As with most resin kits these parts needed casting lugs removing, seams sanding and a thorough cleaning to remove any release agent or grease.

The thickness of the manhole cover and road gully are far greater than their real life counterparts and this forced me to consider how I would construct the base. Whilst I could always sand these parts to a more reasonable thickness, I did want to be able to build the base up a little so that I could allow for recessing the tarmac alley to create some potholes. I would be creating the tarmac finish using *Liquitex Resin Stucco* and to lay this to any great thickness would be cost prohibitive, plus it would take a long time to dry. I did consider building up the thickness using *Celluclay*, but decided that instead some 5mm thick *foamboard* would be easier as it would give me a flat surface onto which the *Stucco* could be trowelled. To give the *foamboard* a neat edge I purchased some plastic angle sections and glued them in place with mitred corners. I did consider

40: completed diorama showing close up of the street furniture and *The Joker*.

using this as the baseboard itself, but felt that the combined weight of all the models would be better served by gluing the *foamboard* to a wooden base.

I scraped the paper covering off the top surface of the *foamboard* so that the foam could be compressed where desired and cut out holes into which I could insert the gully and manhole cover. After leaving the first coat of *Resin Stucco* to dry for twenty-four hours I realised it would need a second coat in places, but before applying this I installed the drainage fittings so that the second coat of *Stucco* could go up to them for a better fit. I also pushed my thumb into several areas to create the potholes and uneven surfaces. Following the second coat of *Stucco* I painted the base an overall matt black and gave the edges of the board a coat of satin varnish. *Woodland Scenics Asphalt Top Coat* is an ideal finish for roads but, to avoid any brush marks and to add a little variation in colour, I applied it to the base with a sponge. The manhole and gully were drybrushed with Boltgun Metal and Raw Sienna.

The concrete barriers were painted *Vallejo* Grey, White and Scarlet; the wheelie bins were painted *Red-Orange* and *Games Workshop* Darksun and the oil drums Olive. With the base colours dry the items were weathered by drybrushing with Raw Sienna and Earth Brown then given a wash with Raw Umber and a quick application of the ubiquitous *Charcoal Woodstain*. The *House Accessories* sets included rainwater pipes, in short sections, which I glued together with a bend at the bottom to use as a rainwater pipe discharging into the gully, and a straight section for use as a soil stack, which, for obvious reasons, would have an underground connection to the mains drains. These pipes were primed and painted Matt Black, followed by some weathering as described above. In order to have some rubbish spilling out of the bins I soaked a paper tissue with a used tea bag (Earl Grey, of course); tore off small sections and draped them over the edge of the bin whilst still damp. I used tissue paper, as anything thicker would be vastly out of scale with the diorama. A few dabs of green wash were added to the paper to complete the rubbish.

The wall panels were glued to the base and the vertical pipes were glued to the wall. The base now needed further detailing and weathering to ensure that it looked like a well-worn alleyway and that the asphalt had been laid up to the building and not the other way round. Rather than try and fill the gap between wall and yard I decided to conceal it with various forms of detritus. I started off with some more torn tissue paper and added some Silver Birch seeds to replicate fallen leaves. The joint was fully hidden with some loose gravel and a little fine green flock to replicate moss. I further dirtied down the yard with *Mig Pigment Powders*. *Light Dusk* was added to the windows, and wiped clean from the centre of the glass. *Industrial City Dirt* and *Dried Mud* were applied to the brickwork and asphalt. Please be aware that the courser the texture of the base you are applying the pigment to the more difficult it is to wipe off – so when applying it to the yard only place it where you want it. I deliberately left streaks clear in the yard to indicate the path the *Batmobile* had taken before it came to a halt. When dry, the pigment was wiped from areas of brickwork and loosened by rubbing a very stiff, old brush on the yard. I decided to apply some of *Woodland Scenics Realistic Water* to replicate some puddles in the potholes in the yard, in the road gully and on top of the oil drums. To break the surface tension of the *Realistic Water* in the potholes I used the leading edge of a palette knife to spread the water about, creating streaks that would have occurred as the car had driven through the puddles. I set the base to one side to allow the water to dry and turned my attention to the figures.

I brushed the dust off the box containing the white metal figures and found that I had already given them a coat of primer many years ago. On closer inspection I noticed that at some point over the years *Batman* had lost the tip from one of his ears, so some epoxy putty came to the rescue and I gave the two figures a quick clean before treating them to a fresh coat of primer. The primer showed a small number of defects that needed filling and, before giving the figures a final coat of primer, I used a very fine saw blade to remove the characters from their bases. This enabled me to drill a hole in the foot of each figure, into which I glued a short section of brass rod which, in turn, allowed me to support each figure in a pin vice so that I could I paint it without holding it.

When it comes to painting figures at this scale you need to use paint that is suitably thinned, not only to help the flow of paint from the brush in tight spaces, but also to ensure that a thick coat of paint does not obscure any details. This causes its own set of problems as the thinned paint tends to be translucent, so I always try to apply a base coat of colour to each area of the model using multiple thin coats of paint to build up the colour. *Games Workshop's Foundation Paints* are quite pigment-intensive and so are ideal for this work. The figure can then be painted without fear of the primer showing through.

The other problem with working with this size of figure is that it is very difficult to blend colours when applying paint with an airbrush. Whilst this can be achieved by hand brushing on oil paints, the long drying time that allows for the blending of colours can be problematic, particularly when working to deadlines. Colour shading can be created by painting slightly different shades of each colour next to each other, but I have recently discovered that *Liquitex* produce a *Flow Extender* that increases the drying time for acrylic paints, allowing for the blending of colours as with oil paints. Whilst you still have to be careful not to smudge the paint as you are working on the model, it can be quickly dried with the application of heat from a hair dryer. I therefore decided to use this technique whilst painting *Batman's* cape.

I used my usual flesh tones for painting the face; Neutral Grey mixed with black for the body suit and Mordian Blue darkened with Payne's Grey and Mars Black for the cape. When I had completed painting the figure I noticed that there was quite a hard line between the cape and body suit that was quite soft sculpturally. Very carefully, I brushed on some dark blue pigment powder at the junction of the two colours made by mixing blue and black pastels to soften the shading, and gave the figure a coat of matt varnish to seal the work.

The *Joker* figure was painted in the appropriate colours, with the white face the most difficult area to complete. If too much shadow is used the face looks grey; not enough and the skin looks like clown's make up. Reviewing the figure I realised that I hadn't got it quite right – it looked more like Cesar Romero than Heath Ledger, which is not helped by the fact that the figure is sculpted with a more traditional appearance including the long-tailed jacket. As the character would be positioned on the periphery of the scene I decided that I could live with it as it was and move on.

All that remained to do to complete the model was to arrange the *Batmobile* and figures on the base.

Woodland Encounter

Converting eight-inch figures and creating a 1/9th scale Tolkien-esque forest clearing

The works of JRR Tolkien have been a big part of my life since I was first introduced to *The Hobbit* in an English lesson at school at the tender age of eleven. Since that time I have read and re-read both *The Hobbit* and *The Lord of the Rings* many times, even managing *The Silmarillion* a couple of times and nibbling at the histories of *Middle Earth*, published since Tolkien's death. The *BBC's* radio plays were magnificent productions that kept the imagination fed until Peter Jackson came along with his magnum opus film trilogy of **The Lord of the Rings**. While watching the films I felt as though the production team had somehow reached into my mind's eye, pulled out my mental images of what *Middle Earth* should look like and presented them on screen for everyone to see. Talking to friends, this seemed to be the case with everyone I spoke to, and I can only put this phenomenon down to the fact that Tolkien was such a good writer, able to evoke almost identical mental images in the minds of his readers.

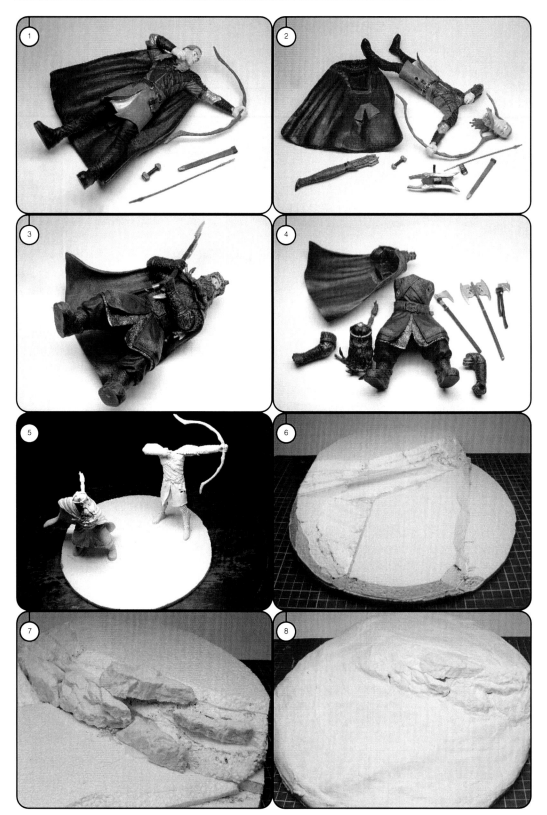

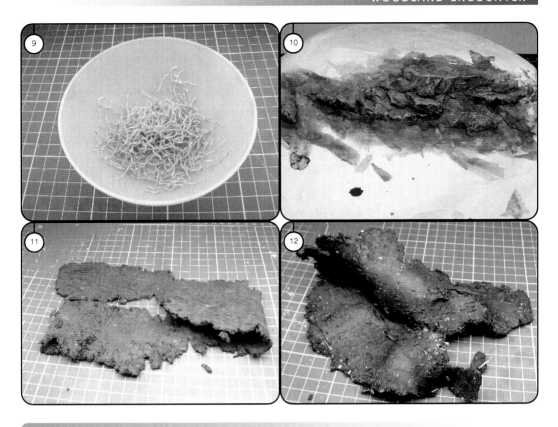

1- 2: *Legolas* figure (and dismantled). 3-4: *Gimli* figure (and dismantled). 5: test pose. 6. foam built up in layers.

7: addition of plaster rocks. 8: plaster bandage added to blend together landscape. 9: tea-stained string.

10: painted rocks. 11: putty earth. 12: putty earth with string added.

When the films were first released a plethora of merchandising was brought out, as is the case with most Hollywood blockbusters these days, and inevitably some of it was better than others. When **The Fellowship of the Ring** was first released *Applause*, a company best known for making 'gift' type items for greetings card shops, released a set of four solid vinyl figures approximately eight inches tall. I don't quite know why they released these characters (other than the obvious ringing of tills), but I can only assume that they were trying to fill a gap between the multitude of small action figures and the high-end collectable statues produced by *Weta Workshop*. Unfortunately, rather than filling that gap the figures seemed to fall between two stools: they were rigid and did nothing other than sit on a shelf and so did not appeal to children – and the paint finish was so poor that the collector end of the market did not really want them on its shelves either. Please bear with me, this is going somewhere, *honest*. Whilst I wanted some **Lord of the Rings** figures for my collection the *Weta* statues were out of my price range and I did not want to play with dolls... sorry... *action figures*. I hadn't bought any of these *Applause* characters as I thought they were too expensive for what they appeared to be and contented myself with the small white metal figures produced by *Games Workshop*, which are very nice, particularly for creating small-scale dioramas, but can be quite wearing on the eyes when you get to a certain age. Speaking of eyes, it was on my return from seeing my ophthalmologist at the local hospital, and as I was walking past one of the aforementioned card shops, that I noticed the *Applause* characters being

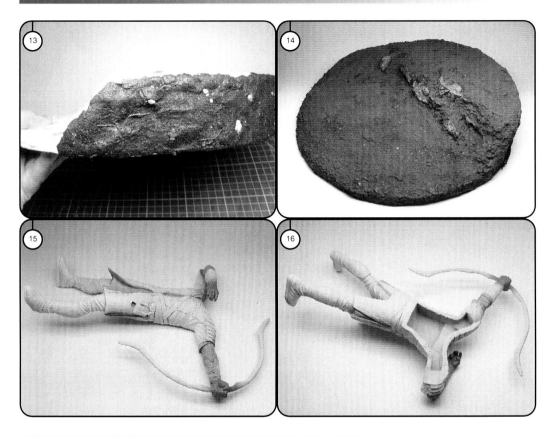

13: earth applied to the base. 14: pre-coloured *Celluclay* added to base.

15-16: *Legolas* primed and shirt painted blue-grey.

sold at drastically reduced prices. Being a sucker for a bargain I decided to take the plunge and brought the set home with me. It was when I got the figures home and started working on them I realised that under an atrocious paint job was a set of really nice sculpts offering plenty of detail and good likenesses to the actors portraying the characters.

These characters were completed in nice time for the release of **The Two Towers** and I was pleased to learn that a second set had been released. I think that the card shops were being cautious, however, as they did not stock the full range... I eventually found *Legolas* and *Treebeard* in a *Forbidden Planet* in Liverpool, and it wasn't until many years later that I discovered a *Gimli* in a Tolkien shop in Holland via the Internet. One of the things I have noticed in recent years is that major kit manufacturers are producing less and less film tie-in models, particularly on the figure side, presumably as the kit building hobby, as a whole, is on the decline, and there have been a lot of pre-painted statues produced. To a certain extent I can understand this, as there will be a lot of people out there who do not have the skills or the time to create a model to display standard, and there is an attraction to being able to pull a ready-built and painted model out of the box. Whilst I am sure that most people reading this book would prefer to build and paint something for themselves, these 'pre-paints' can be a source for models that have not been produced in kit form. It was whilst I was bandying about ideas for a 1:9 scale diorama for this book that I remembered the *Applause* figures and decided that they would be ideal for a forest-based diorama.

Models made of hard vinyl such as these have their advantages and disadvantages. On the plus side no filling and sanding is required, other than the careful removal of the cast-in copyright notice, and parts fit is very tight. On the down side it is virtually impossible to remove the seam line, as hard vinyl does not sand well at all. Fortunately the seam is mostly hidden on these figures, except for an obvious line across the top of their capes. I tried to remove this by using a sharp, new scalpel blade with a curved edge (*Swann Morton* type 15): inevitably some of the detail was lost, but it was not unacceptable. Before working on figures such as these consideration needs to be given as to how best to prepare them. I began by disassembling the characters simply by pulling them apart. As they are made of hard vinyl and have simple male and female joints which have been glued together they come apart relatively easily with a little brute force and the judicious application of a hair dryer to soften the parts – although care has to be taken where the vinyl is thin as it can easily tear if too much force is applied.

A decision has to be made at this point as to whether to strip off the existing paintwork or work on top of what's already there. To some extent this is down to personal preference, how thickly the existing paint has been applied and to what extent the paint obscures the underlying detail. In this instance I decided to work over the existing paint job as the paint had been applied fairly thinly and the parts had been cast in coloured vinyl, so stripping the paint would not give me the advantage of working from a consistent base colour. What I did do was give the parts a very thorough clean using a stiff toothbrush, some *Cif* cream cleaner and hot, soapy water. When dry the parts were given a coat of Grey Primer to totally cover the different colours and provide a key for the subsequent paintwork, this being followed by a mist coat of White Primer. I prefer white as a base colour when painting flesh tones as most flesh colours are slightly translucent and I feel that a grey base can dull the finished colour.

I knew that the techniques I was going to use on the base would need reasonable drying times between operations so I thought I had best start work on it before progressing with the figures. As I have mentioned elsewhere in this book the secret to choosing a good base for a diorama is to have one big enough to fit everything you want in the scene onto and not look too crowded, but not so big that there are areas of dead space that are not doing anything. The other thing about bases is to ensure that you can provide a nice final presentation and I have found that wooden cutting boards of various sizes are a relatively cheap source. Comparing the size of the figures to the sizes of board I had available to me I decided that a base of 300mm diameter would work well. Because I was going to be using a number of wet techniques for building the base I did not want to work directly off the wooden cutting board as it could cause the wood to warp, so I cut out an appropriately-sized circle from 6mm thick polystyrene as supplied by *Woodland Scenics*. I find that scrap polystyrene from packaging can be useful when building up ground levels, but it can be a little on the soft side... the *WS* polystyrene, however, is very dense and my preferred choice.

The polystyrene can be cut with an old carving knife, but it does tend to break up and leave a lot of loose particles and rough edges. The best way to cut polystyrene is to use a hot knife or wire and many of these are commercially available. However, in an attempt to be frugal (or tight-fisted, as some might put it) I decided to literally use a hot knife. Before I go any further I should say that this is a dangerous procedure and should only be carried out by a responsible adult taking great care. Having a gas cooker, I determined to use this as my source of heat and the adjacent worktop as my work area, although you will need to ensure that you have a non-flammable cover over the worktop as you are likely to ruin it if you are not careful. Using an old, and I do mean old – as in you are never going to use it for anything else afterwards – wooden handled butter knife (wooden, as it acts as a heat insulator... use an all metal knife and you wont be able to hold it), place the knife in the naked flame until it starts to get hot. It will then slice through the polystyrene like – well – like a knife through butter. The big difference is that when a knife goes through butter it does not have hot, molten polystyrene stuck to it that can drip off and result in a nasty injury if you're not careful. The difference between using a commercially available product and my 'cheap and cheerful' method is that the commercial hot knife has a continuous source of heat whereas mine cools quickly and as soon as it stops cutting you need to put it back into the flame to re-heat it. You may find that you get a bit of polystyrene stuck to your knife that catches light when returned to the flame – please wait until this extinguishes itself before proceeding as we don't want to start any fires. I'm sorry if I sound like your mother for repeating myself, but please be careful if you are going to use this technique and if you have any doubts stick to the cold bread knife. It's always better to be safe than sorry.

Rather than just having a flat base I wanted to raise some of the levels for a couple of reasons. Firstly, as this is a two-figure diorama I wanted to have one of the figures on a raised area so that the second did not obscure the view of the first. Secondly, when you have a diorama that has a more distinct front and back view it can be helpful from a visual perspective to create a horizon line.

With the polystyrene cut out I test-fitted the figures onto the base and pencilled in where I wanted them to go. I then started sketching on rough ideas of contour lines and level changes before physically building them. I find it helpful to use a very soft pencil when sketching on polystyrene as it does not damage the surface as a hard pencil or pen would. I then went back to the kitchen and built up the layers with more polystyrene glued in place with a hot glue gun. Not only did the hot knife enable me to cut the polystyrene to size, but I was able to chamfer the edges of the board to give more suitable level changes. I left some gaps as I wanted to add some rock faces at the main level change.

The rock faces were cast in plaster using *Woodland Scenics Rock Moulds*. When mixing up plaster you will probably have more plaster left than you intended so it is always useful to have a spare mould to hand that you use the excess plaster in. You might not need the extra cast now, but it can be saved in a plastic container and used on another project. The plaster takes about half an hour to set and can be released from the mould by giving it a gentle tap on the back, although you may find that some of the thinner rock shapes break as they are removed from the mould, but these can be glued back together or used separately. I selected a number of rock shapes and hot glued them in place with some scrap polystyrene behind, where necessary, to fill any unwanted voids.

17: painted tunic. 18: browns added to straps and tunic detail painted.

19: boot detail. 20: base flesh and shadow wash.

To try and make the surface more even and regularly contoured I added some plaster-soaked bandages, which are readily available from the Model Railway section of your local model shop. These come on a roll and are cut to size before giving them a quick soak in water and placing them on the model. The bandages are overlapped and smoothed out using your fingers. Once you are satisfied with the ground levels you will need to set the base to one side for a day or two to let it thoroughly dry out. When the base was dry I coloured the plaster rocks by adding washes of Yellow Ochre, Burnt Umber and Black, all from the *Woodland Scenics Liquid Pigment* range and all applied with a foam brush. These pigments dry fairly quickly and I realised that I wasn't satisfied with the finish so I gently drybrushed on some Unbleached Titanium White then returned with the pigment washes, but this time adding some Raw Umber and Stone Grey, which is a sort of green-grey. The main thing to remember when using these pigment washes is to work quickly so that the colours are applied wet on wet, as the colours will blend where they overlap and create a more natural appearance. It is also worth noting that it you mix up more of these washes than you need you can cover them with cling film and they will keep in the fridge for many weeks.

As I've mentioned in other chapters I like to create dioramas that can be seen in the round, even if they have an obvious front and back. This meant that I needed to consider how I was going

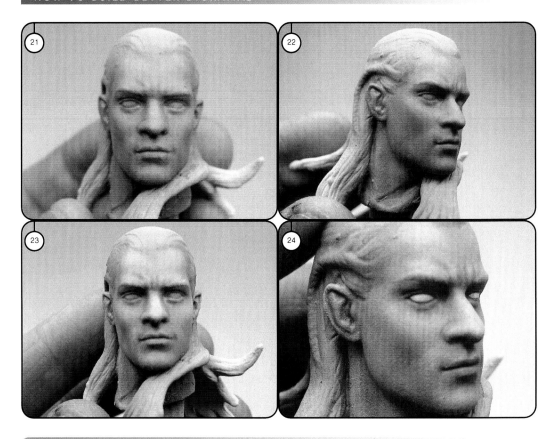

21:base colour drybrushed to emphasise shadows. 22 highlights added.
23: shadow wash added to lines and crevices of the face. 24: white added to eyes.

to treat the raised vertical faces to the edge of the base. I could have just painted them matt black, but I do like to make life difficult for myself and decided to, in effect, create a section through the ground showing soil, rocks, roots and the like. The first stage in this process would be to create some roots – and to do so I would need string. I cut up short lengths of string and placed them in a bowl with a tea bag, and made some tea – Earl Grey. Hot, of course. I left the string to soak in the tea overnight so that it would become stained, and for this reason you must use natural fibre string and not a nylon type as it will not absorb the tea. The other thing that happens as the string soaks in the tea is that the fibres start to loosen and you can unwind it to expose the finer fibres. It's only as I write that last sentence that I realise why we sometimes get strange looks from non-modellers. Imagine the scenario: you go into work of a morning and a colleague asks you what you did last night and you reply, 'Oh, I had my evening meal; washed the dishes; took the dog for a walk and sat unwinding short lengths of string that I had dyed in cold tea whilst watching an episode of **Voyage to the Bottom of the Sea**.'

When the string was dry I set about making my subterranean earth mix which, because it was going to be applied to a vertical surface, would need to be much thicker than one of my usual mixes to avoid any slump. The basis of my mix was to be *Milliput* two-part epoxy putty and, as I wanted it to be self-coloured, I decided to combine the Terracotta and Black varieties to try and create a dirty brown colour. I have to admit that I'd had the packets of *Milliput* for quite a while and, unfortunately, they had gotten stiff with age (I know the feeling) and were going to be hard work to mix together properly so that the putty would cure correctly. To make life easier I pulled off the shelf the pasta-making machine that I had bought for modelling purposes only and fed the two component parts of each colour of putty through the rollers. This was repeated half a dozen or so times with a little hand-kneading in between to get each putty thoroughly mixed and blended together. I then put the two colours of putty together and repeated the process until I ended up with a flat sheet of something that looked like you had scrapped it off the bottom of your shoe. I next added the string fibres in between layers of putty and put it through the rollers a couple of times to mix it all in, subsequently repeating the process with some dried herbs. At the end of this, other than the nice smell from the herbs, it really did look like something you had trodden in – but it *is* supposed to be lucky, so I could only hope it held good omens for the completion of the model. I should note here that cleaning the putty residue from the pasta machine is a bit of a pain in the bum, but it is important that you keep the rollers clean as the machine does come in very useful when you need a flat sheet of putty of an even thickness.

By now time had progressed and I could feel the putty was starting to cure, so I needed to work quickly to get it onto the base in time. Because the putty was in flat strips applying it to the base was very straightforward and it followed the contours nicely. As a final touch I pressed a few small stones into the putty and sprinkled on some *Woodland Scenics Earth* and *Soil Scatters* using a jar for storing herbs that has a perforated top. This was all fixed in place with a coat of diluted PVA glue sprayed on using a pump bottle from the local hobby shop and left to dry overnight.

It was now time to add some soil to the forest floor using *Celluclay*, which is a pre-shredded papier-mâché type product. Rather than just mixing it with water I added some PVA glue to try and avoid shrinkage cracks. I also pre-coloured the water before mixing in the *Celluclay* using *Woodland Scenics Earth Pigment* darkened with some Slate Grey so that the finished product had a consistent colour throughout, rather than a surface colour that the white of the *Celluclay* could peep through. The *Celluclay* was then applied to the base with an artist's palette knife, using a small one to work it in around the stones; a larger one for around the edges, and a butter knife to spread it over the large, open areas. Once complete it was allowed to dry for three days before any more work was done on the base. Unless you are a very good guesser, you will have probably made more *Celluclay* than you need for a project. Fear not, as the mix will keep in the fridge if covered with cling film, and should it dry out you should be able to re-activate it by adding a little water.

Whilst the base was drying I turned my attention to painting the figures. I had decided to brush paint them as airbrushing and masking the complex paint schemes would be a pain in the bum. The other reason for hand painting was that most of the surfaces are highly textured and the process of drybrushing would emphasise the texture more that just using the airbrush. The majority of the paints used for the two figures come from the *Vallejo* range of colours, which is probably one of the best ranges of paint for hand brushing as they flow nicely and most cover extremely well. For each colour I tended to follow a specific procedure – a base colour was painted that was slightly darker than the final colour I wanted for the overall appearance. This was followed by the actual colour, and this was drybrushed to help accentuate the texture of the parts

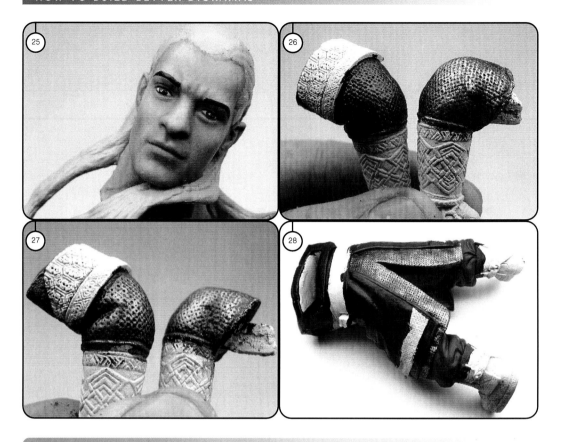

25: face complete and hair base colour applied. 26: *Gimli* – (left) base colour and (right) metallic drybrush applied.

27: completed chainmail. 28: base colours added to *Gimli* torso and legs. 29: further browns added.

30: torso almost completed. 31-32: torso, leg and boot details.

and leave natural shadows in the recessed areas. A lighter shade was then drybrushed over the raised areas to create highlights. A wash was created using a much darker shade and this was run into any seams in the material and any junction between different areas of colour. One of the other advantages of the *Vallejo* range is that the paints are one of only a few acrylic ranges that actually dry to a true matt finish.

I started work on *Legolas* by painting his shirt a pale blue-grey, created by mixing Azure with Pale Blue (which is actually closer to a pale turquoise) as a base colour, darkened by adding more Azure and a drop of Black, and lightened by adding more Pale Blue. The trousers were based on Dark Blue Grey, and the boots on US Dark Green (which is a very useful green-grey). The boots feature some engraved markings and, as these were not obvious on the reference photographs I had to hand, I just ran a dark brown wash into them. The tunic was also based on the US Dark Green, but varied by adding greens and browns to it, the engravings on the tunic being emphasised with a wash of Tan Yellow. Not having a lot of *Vallejo* browns in my paint box, and not wanting to go out to the shops at ten to three on a Sunday afternoon, I pulled out some *Games Workshop* Dark Flesh (which is a great leather brown) and their Scorched

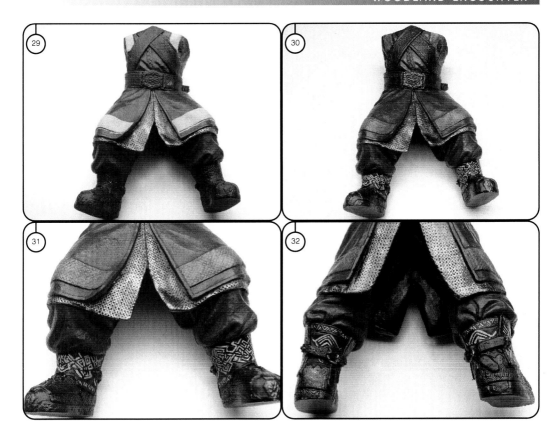

Brown for the belts and straps. The acrylics from *Games Workshop* also work very well for hand brushing, but do dry with that slight sheen you get from most acrylic paints. These were given a black wash and drybrushed with some Raw Sienna to give the leather a worn appearance.

For the buckles and other metallic features I used Liquid Gold Leaf, which gives a strong, natural gold colour. The down side to this product is that you need to keep it constantly stirred – or shaken if that's your preference, *Mr. Bond* – to stop the pigment and carrier from separating. You will also need to clean your brush with white spirit or similar, so I keep one brush dedicated to the application of this stuff. On reflection, I decided that the Gold was a little too bright and toned it down with a wash of Raw Umber.

For the flesh I went down a slightly different route than that used for the other acrylic colours. I have to admit that the airbrush has to be my tool of choice when applying flesh tones, but I wanted to try and keep to purely brush techniques for this project. I had previously laid down a base flesh tone as I like to work from the inside out when painting figures, but I had not gone any further with the flesh colours as I was trying to avoid any masking on this job and I realised that there might be some overspill from adjacent colours. Fortunately, this had been kept to a minimum, so a minor touch up with my base flesh colour gave me a good place to start rendering the skin.

As with other projects in this book I used my standard flesh mix of *Liquitex* Raw Sienna, Burnt Sienna and Titanium White. This was darkened with Raw Umber, Burnt Umber and a little more

Burnt Sienna. The base flesh colour was lightened by adding Unbleached Titanium White and Raw Sienna. By the time I had finished mixing the paint I had a base colour, two shade tones and three light tones. Onto the base flesh I washed the lighter of my two shade tones using a scrubbing motion with my brush to try and soften the edges. This was liberally applied to all the recessed areas on the face and hands and once it had dried I drybrushed the base colour to tidy up the edges and reduce the extents of the shadow. I then worked through the three highlight colours, reducing the amount I drybrushed with each colour until the lightest tone was only applied to the nose, top of the cheeks, chin and brows. Drybrushed paint has to be applied with a light touch to build up the colour as, with the best will in the world, you are likely to end up with a powdery type appearance. Fortunately I was reasonably satisfied with the results, but to tie all the colours together and minimise any powder effects I applied a flesh-coloured filter, which is a fancy way of saying a very thin wash covering the whole area. When the filter was dry I used a fine brush to apply the two shade tones in a wash to the deeply recessed and lined areas such as the brow, around the eyes and under the nose. A Raw Umber wash was run between the lips and the lip colour was created by adding Red Oxide to the base colour, again applied as a wash. The whites of the eyes were created by using Titanium White and Raw Umber added to flesh, lightened for the centres of the eyes with some additional White. Raw Umber was mixed with Payne's Grey to provide the top eyelash and block in the iris, which was coloured with the addition of some Pale Blue. The pupil was created using black paint on the end of a toothpick and the eyes were finished with a coat of gloss varnish.

I painted the capes for both *Legolas* and *Gimli* at the same time, as they are both the same colour, using US Dark Green as a base and highlighting it with some Light Grey added to the base colour. Rather than using a wash for the shade tones because of the large surface areas involved I used some dark green-grey pastel powder, which was fixed with a coat of matt varnish. The leaf-shaped broach was painted *Games Workshop* Mithril Silver and, once dry, *Tamiya* Clear Green was used to complete the decoration.

With the paintwork complete I re-assembled the body parts using non-fogging superglue to ensure that it was not adversely affected by the curing of the adhesive. The arrow that came with the model was also cast in hard vinyl but, because of its thin cross-section, was positively limp. I therefore cut the ends off and replaced the shaft with some brass rod to make it rigid (there's probably a double entendre or two that could have been made in that sentence, but I'll leave it up to your imagination). The bow obviously needed stringing, but I realised that anything that would put tension on the bow would cause it to deform as the vinyl was not strong enough, so I created two sections of 'string' from very fine brass rod and glued them in place, this also helping support the upper section of the bow, which did have a tendency to droop. Before setting *Legolas* to one side I applied a little weathering to his boots and the bottom edges of his cape and tunic by dry brushing some Neutral Grey and Raw Umber.

With the *Celluclay* dry it was time to put down some ground cover. This is a messy process so I suggest that you work on the draining board of your sink, or somewhere else you can easy wipe down and clean afterwards. Alternatively, spread plenty of old newspapers over your work area and its surrounds. When modelling terrain you need to carry out as much research as you would for any other kind of model. Obviously books are still a good source of reference, but a nice walk in the countryside will probably give you as much, if not more, inspiration – and it's good for you. I used various different materials to create the ground cover, which needs to be attached using a spray-applied PVA glue. Unfortunately using a brush will disturb any scatter you have just laid. *Woodland Scenics Scenic Cement* is ideal for this and can be applied using their own spray bottle, or a pump action spray bottle available from craft shops, that gives a much finer spray, or a

33-34: completed *Gimli* head. 35-36: ground cover randomly applied to base. 37-38: the completed base with bracken.

combination of both as needs be. All the various types of scatter were laid in a random pattern, allowing the different colours and textures to show through. Each layer of scatter is covered with another layer of glue, which fixes that layer in place and provides adhesion for the next layer. When all the scatter is laid the base is given another coat of glue to finally fix everything in place.

I started off by sprinkling on some *Woodland Scenics Fine Turf Soil,* followed by a mix of *Soil* and *Earth* to act as a transition to the areas where I scattered the *Earth Fine Turf* on its own. As well as creating a good base layer for the deadfall it also visually tied in with the *Soil* and *Earth* that had been sprinkled on the sides. What follows will read like some bizarre recipe as I raided the dried herb and spice rack of my local supermarket for the deadfall – not only do such ingredients work well visually, but they are relatively cheap – especially compared to the price of various scatters produced for the Model Railway hobby.

Italian seasoning was scattered on first: this has the appearance of fine crushed leaves in a mixture of green, red and brown colours. This was followed by Thyme, which is green in colour and looks a bit like scale dead grass, and then some Herbes de Provence, which have the appearance of crushed green leaves. Taking a break from the culinary delights I sprinkled on some scatter from *Faller*, which I think is called *Ploughed Earth*, but I cannot be sure as I lost the header card to the pack. This works well as the kind of scatter you find around the base of plants so I limited it to the areas where I intended to plant bushes. Back to the spice rack, and I sparingly applied some Whole Cloves, which look like small twigs. I limited their use as I felt that they could become too intrusive if overused, and I didn't particularly like the smell. The Cloves were followed by some Whole Cumin and Rosemary, which look like very fine twigs in brown and green respectively. The ground cover was completed by using some Silver Birch seeds, which look like very small leaves. These can be bought commercially from hobby suppliers or sourced directly from Silver Birch trees when you go on that country walk for your research. The size of the Silver Birch seeds means that they look most to scale at about 1:12 through 1:35 – at any smaller scale they look too big and at any larger scale they look too small, so I was just on the border of them looking realistic, but I think they work in context. The Silver Birch seeds were laid in areas where dead leaves might accumulate, such as recesses and around the base of planting, with a few drifting over the rest of the ground.

By this time I had collected a soggy mess of not-so-dried herbs around the base, particularly Thyme for some reason. I then applied this mash to the perimeter of the base around the raised areas of ground to cover the transition from

Celluclay ground to the *Milliput* earth. This was then set-aside for another couple of days to let it dry thoroughly before starting to plant some bushes.

Whilst the base was drying again I decided to paint *Gimli*. Looking at my reference photographs I realised that *Gimli* was going to be an exercise in monochromatic painting – everything was to be a shade of brown – and that I would need to keep the model visually interesting and the different materials distinct from one another using what can be a dull colour. I had made a trip to the *Manchester Modelzone* and picked up various shades of brown from the *Vallejo* range: German Camouflage Black Brown (that's a name that really trips off the tongue); Burnt Umber (which looks more like Raw Umber to me – but what do I know?); Flat Brown and Red Leather. In the order listed the browns started off very dark and got lighter and redder. These four colours, in conjunction with some Tan Yellow I already had in my paint box, formed the basis of all the colours on the figure, with me mixing them together to create the necessary light and dark tones of each colour.

The process of painting *Gimli* followed the procedures I had used for painting *Legolas*, so I won't repeat myself (that makes a change, I'm sure I hear you say), but *will* mention a couple of points. Because I was working monochromatically I laid down all the base colours first rather than going through the base-shade-highlight process for each colour in turn, as I had for *Legolas*. I then went through the application of shade and highlight for each shade of brown. By doing this I was able to be more economical with the paint, as I could place all the colours on my pallet at the same time to mix the necessary shade and highlight tones, as a highlight colour for a dark brown could be used as a shade tone for a light brown.

Gimli's clothing features a lot of metallic trim and I painted this with *Games Workshop* Burnished Gold using a drybrushing technique, as most of this trim was a raised detail on the model. Some of this patterning was repeated on the boots, but was flush with the adjacent leather and so drybrushing would not have been appropriate. I realised that the only way to apply the trim would be to individually paint in all the detail. Knowing that metallic colours tend to apply best when drybrushed or airbrushed I decided to use the Tan Yellow as I knew that it could be added nicely with just one coat, and for the sake of my tired eyes I realised that one coat had to be preferable to going over fine detail multiple times. Whilst I appreciated that this would have a different appearance to the rest of the trim once it was weathered I felt that it would not stick out like a sore thumb, and it was sufficiently far away from similar trim that had been finished with the metallic colour not to jar visually.

For *Gimli*'s flesh colours I used the same tones as I had for *Legolas*, but added a little Raw Umber to tone them down slightly. I also used the shadow washes a little more to emphasise the wrinkles and creases in the skin. I chose *Games Workshop* metallic colours for the weaponry, starting off with Tin Bitz, and my own mix of Boltgun Metal and Chaos Black, and working my way through to a highlight colour of Chainmail. The handles were painted black (as a change from all that brown), and the handles and blades given a little wear by drybrushing with Raw Sienna. With all the paintwork complete the figure was re-assembled.

With the base dry and the figures complete I carried out a final test pose before applying some foliage to the scene. I had originally considered using a dead branch from one of those country walks as a tree trunk (if you are going to do this let the branch dry out and acclimatise before fixing to the base as there is always the potential for mould growth if used damp and the timber can warp and move as it dries out), but I realised that it could dominate the scene if I was not careful and draw attention away from the figures. I therefore decided to just keep to dense bushes and let the fallen leaves imply the forest location.

When I was happy with *Gimli* and *Legolas'* position I worked out which areas would need planting and set about creating my bushes. One of my first thoughts had been to use *Woodland Scenics* plastic tree armatures for the bushes and apply foliage to them, but the plastic was not flexible enough to position the trees close enough together to get the appearance of overgrown hedgerows. Not wanting to put a dent in *Woodland Scenics'* profit margin I used another of their products, called *Fine Leaf Foliage*. This comprises of fine, coloured foam pre-glued to semi-flexible branches, and comes in a range of colours. The foam can be broken off the branches and glued to armatures or the branches themselves can be used as part of the planting – and this is what I did. I used three different colours of foliage – Olive Green, Light Green and Dead Foliage – to provide an appearance of natural variation. To 'plant' each bush I created a hole by pushing a bradawl or *Philips* head screwdriver into the base. The dried *Celluclay* is very robust so a degree of force is required to puncture the 'skin', but, once through, the foam is easy to penetrate. The *Fine Leaf Foliage* is then separated into appropriately sized 'bushes' and the stems coated in PVA glue and pushed into the holes in the *Celluclay*. This process was repeated until I was happy with the arrangement. I finished off the planting by adding a little overgrown grass (another *Woodland Scenics* product) applied in the same way as the bushes.

I realised that I could not just simply glue the two figures to the base as the ground cover would never allow a good mating surface for the glue between the base of the feet of the figures and the surface of the base. I was cautious about scraping away small areas of ground cover as I did not want it to look too obvious that that was the case. I therefore decided to repeat the same process I had undertaken for planting the bushes: I drilled holes in the figures' feet and superglued in place some brass rod with a good length left protruding. Holes were then punched in the base and plenty of PVA applied to the feet of the figures and the brass rod before inserting them into the base.

And there we have it – another diorama completed, and one that, perhaps, shows us that we should look under the surface and consider the potential of an object before dismissing it.

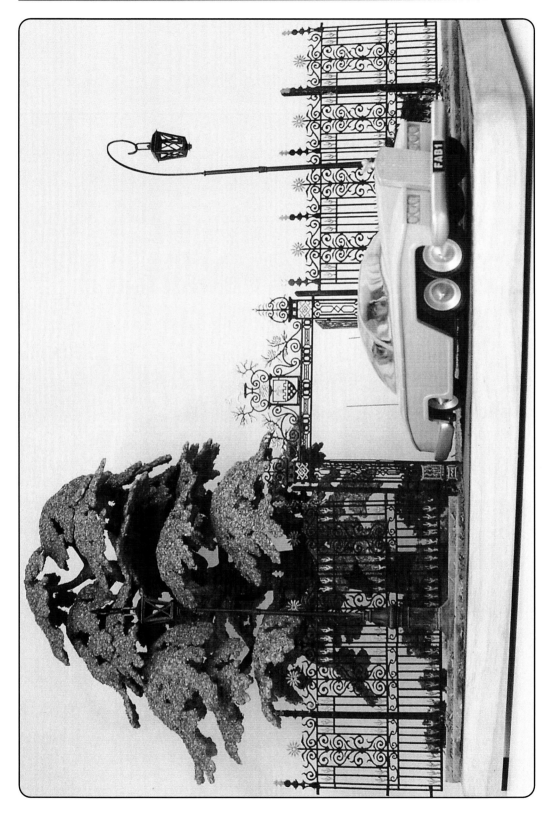

All Quiet on the Rescue Front

Creating a stately and striking
1/32nd scale Thunderbirds scene

have a confession to make – I'm an addict. It started innocently enough when I was young. I'd enjoy the odd one, then sometimes it would be many years before I'd indulge in another. But then, when they became readily available, I could get through four in one go and work my way through a full pack in a matter of days. And it didn't stop there – I started to explore other outlets to get my fix, spending money with wild abandon in order to feed the habit. My name is Barry Ford – I am a **Thunderbirds** fan.

As a change of pace from the many dramatic rescues *International Rescue* gets involved with, I thought, as the subject of this chapter, I would build a quiet scene of *Lady Penelope* and *Parker* leaving the *Creighton-Ward* estate in *FAB 1* and going for a little drive in the country.

For many years since the 1960s *Imai* produced a 1/32nd scale model of *FAB 1* that, whilst it had the basic contours about right, was sadly lacking in many ways – in particular the clear blue canopy... didn't they realise that it clashed with the pink bodywork? The other serious deficit was the interior of the car, minimalistically represented by a flat sheet of plastic onto which *Parker* and *Penny's* heads were stuck. Other items of annoyance were the large missiles launched through the headlights and the general appearance of a toy you glued together, rather than of a scale replica.

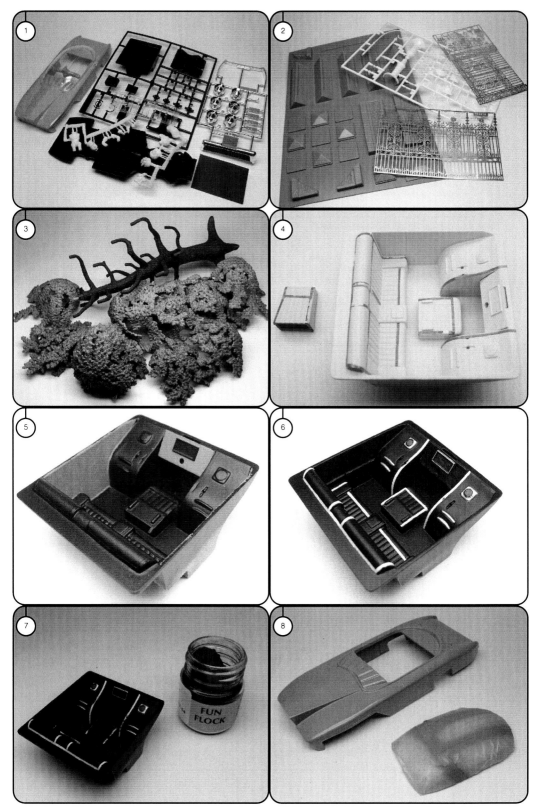

In the late 1990s *Imai* decided to make amends and release a more accurate replica of *FAB 1* that included a full interior, clear canopy, revised bodywork and hubcaps and correctly detailed headlights that could be shown with or without the appropriate machine gun. As a separate item *Imai* also released a set of in-scale *Penelope* and *Parker* resin figures that could be sat in the car's interior. In this chapter I will be using these models in conjunction with a 1/35th scale set of *Park Accessories* from *MiniArt* and some etched brass gates and railings, supplemented with an assortment of Model Railway scenery items.

I decided to paint *FAB 1* prior to assembling it and realised that the only sub-assembly I could make was that formed by gluing together the two halves of the back of *Parker*'s chair. Whilst the appropriate parts were supplied chrome plated I chose to change their appearance for two reasons. Firstly, these parts had some quite noticeable seams that needed sanding down, particularly on the front and rear bumpers, which are refugees from the original kit moulds (the sanding, of course, removes the chrome plating). The other reason I decided to replace the chrome finish was that, as supplied, it just looks too toy-like. Whilst you can fully strip the chrome from the plastic before painting I have found that satisfactory results can be obtained by simply ensuring that any blemishes are sanded smooth then applying a coat of primer over the chromed plastic.

1: *Imai* kit parts. 2: etched brass railings and lamppost parts. 3: *Schleich* tree kit. 4: *FAB1* interior sprayed white and masked.

5: interior painted black and base wood colour. 6: interior painting completed. 7: carpet area covered with red flock.

8: pink paint applied to car body. 9-10: *Penelope* and *Parker* figures are primed.

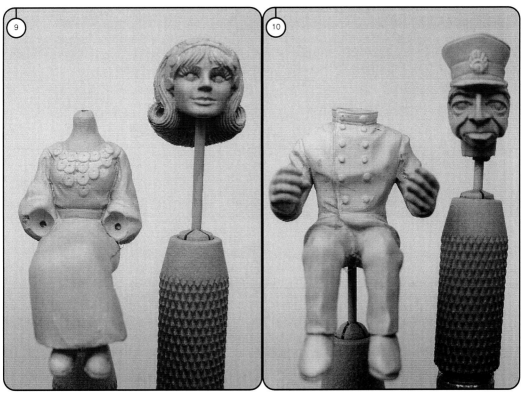

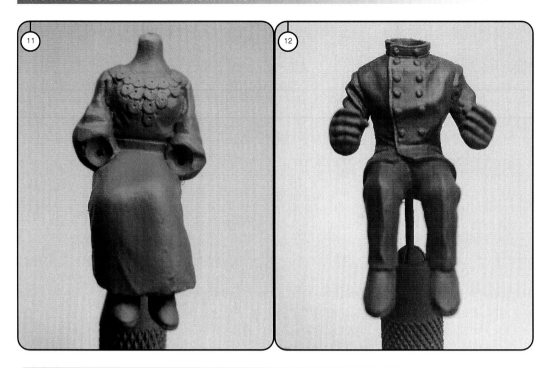

11-12: *Penelope* and *Parker* are given a base coat – blue and brown respectively.

13-14: lighter and darker shades of base colours blended together.

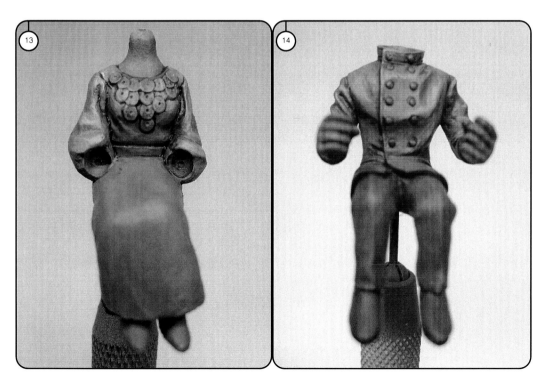

15-16: the completed *Parker*.

17-18: the completed *Penelope*.

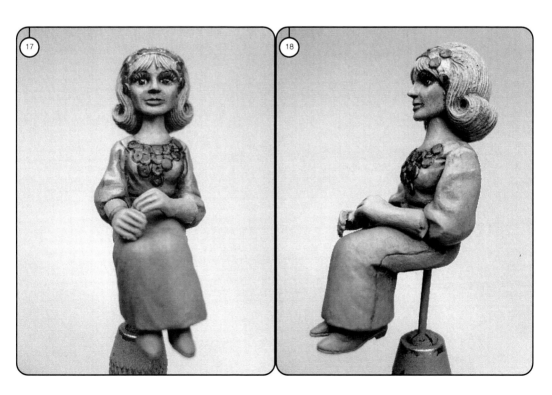

Lacquer-based paints are available to create a very realistic metallic finish. However, lacquers do tend to give off a very strong odour and I did not wish to be coughing and choking from the fumes as I was working, so I plumped for *Vallejo* Chrome, a paint that offers a satisfactory finish with all the advantages of an acrylic. Before applying this I filled the hole in the radiator, intended for another machine gun, with epoxy putty and sanded the area smooth.

I wanted a duller and darker metallic finish for the underside of the car and therefore made *Games Workshop*'s Boltgun Metal, which is a perennial favourite of mine for metallic finishes, my paint of choice. For the bodywork there was really only one paint to go with: *Tamiya*'s Gloss Pink. I must admit I do not know why *Tamiya* produce this colour, as most of their paints are based on military colours, but it is ideal for *FAB 1*. As with all gloss finishes you need to make sure that you have a pristine base, as any defects will be immediately obvious. You will also need to ensure that the paint is suitably thinned and applied in several coats to obtain the desired finish. The clear canopy was masked off and the pink stripes applied in this manner. I realise that the 'real' *FAB 1* has silver trim to its canopy framing but, after careful consideration, I felt that I would obtain a neater finish by just leaving the framing pink rather than applying the silver by either masking or free-hand painting as, scaled down, the silver stripes would be less than a millimetre wide. After

19- 22: completed *FAB 1* interior with *Penelope* and *Parker*. 23: tree prepared by applying *Flexibark* over join. 24: trial layout. 25: cardboard strips added to base to provide a level edge. 26: *resin stucco* trowel applied to base. 27: straight edge scraped over surface to level *stucco*. 28: *Gesso* complete. 29: brass gate and fence.

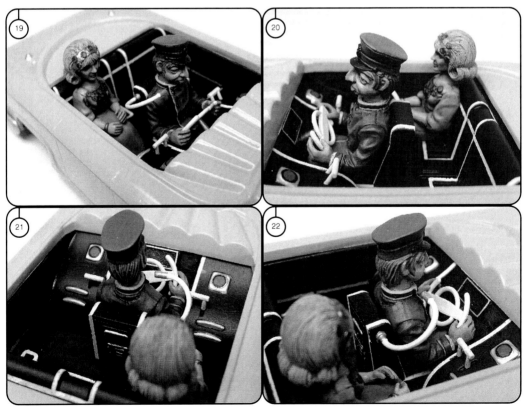

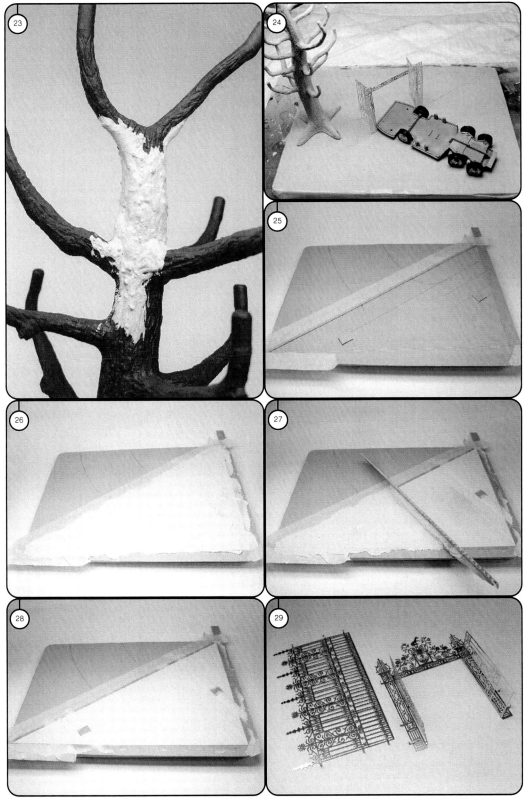

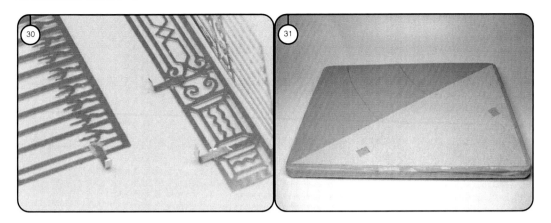

letting the gloss paint dry thoroughly I masked off the body in order to apply the silver stripe down the side with more of the *Vallejo* Chrome Silver.

The underside of the car was given a brush on/wipe off treatment using *Liquitex Charcoal Woodstain* to weather it slightly – I did not go overboard with weathering this area as I couldn't see *Parker* letting the car get into a state of disrepair, and, on a more practical basis, it is never likely to be seen. The wheels were fixed in place as per the instructions and the sub-assembly set aside whilst I turned my attention to the car's interior.

I painted the interior matt white, which I could then mask with very thin masking tape before applying *Liquitex* Mars Black to the seating. When the masking tape is removed the white piping to the seats is complete, although a little touch up may be required to re-cover any paint seepage. To replicate the timber panels I applied a couple of coats of ochre to cover the black, although this does not need to be perfect as any variation in colour will just make it look more natural in appearance. There are many ways of creating a wood grain effect, but in this instance I used *Vallejo's Woodgrain* paint, which is a transparent brown colour. You do need to remember to apply the paint in one direction only and this can be done by using a thin brush and adding one grain at a time. In my case I used an old, small, flat brush that had lost most of its bristles, with most of the paint removed from the brush before application.

To replicate the carpet on the floor of the interior the kit supplies the modeller with a piece of red textured cardboard that needs to be cut to size. Considering my options for a short period I was prompted to exclaim, 'Oh, flock it!' Please let me assure you that I have not just made a spelling mistake or uttered a euphemism. Flock is a collection of small, loose fibres that have been dyed to a particular colour and can be applied to create a soft, textured finish. I carefully applied diluted *PVA* glue to the floor of the car interior ensuring that none went anywhere else, as flock does tend to get everywhere and, even without glue, can stick like the proverbial brown bodily substance to a blanket. Ample flock was spread into the interior and pressed into place using a cotton bud. After allowing the glue to dry adequately any excess flock was emptied out of the interior and retained for future re-use. You will probably find many loose fibres left behind, which are best removed using a dampened cotton bud. In order to minimise any more free-flying flock I gave the interior an overall coat of matt varnish followed by satin varnish to the 'wood' areas. I applied some metallic medium to the view screens to give the black a reflective quality and finished them off with a coat of gloss varnish.

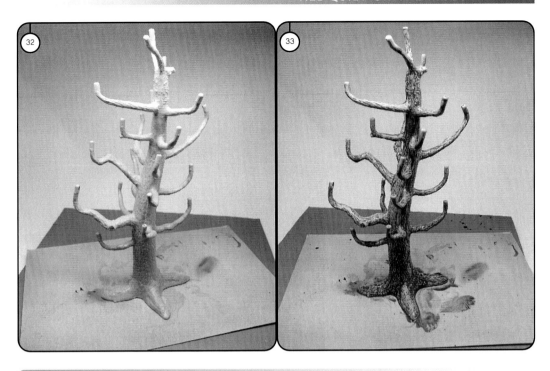

30: brass brackets are glued to railings with superglue. 31: masking is removed from base.

32: Yellow Ochre wash applied to tree. 33: Raw Umber wash added. 34: finally, a Stone Grey wash is added.

35: the completed tree minus foliage.

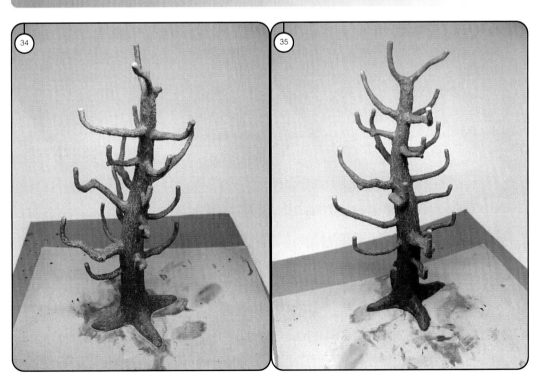

36: asphalt coloured and edging stones added. 37: washes applied to plinth and edgings. 38: first drybrush coat added to plinth and edgings. 39: pavement with first coat of paint applied. 40: completed plinth. 41: items glued to base; earth works commence. 42: paving close-up. 43: earth added to base of tree. 44: soil mix sprinkled on base. 45: foliage and leaves. 46: foliage with leaves glued on and left to dry. 47: soil coloured.

With the sub-assemblies of the car complete I glued them together as per the instructions, although I left off the steering wheel and microphone in order to make life easier when positioning the *Parker* figure later – big fingers and small parts do not a happy combination make.

The *Penny* and *Parker* figures were carefully removed from their sprues whilst I maintained a slow and steady breathing rhythm as I had visions of these tiny parts going flying, to be lost forever in the depths of the carpet. I constructed the bodies, but left off *Penny's* arms and head and *Parker's* head for ease of painting. So that these parts could be handled easily I drilled a small hole in them and glued a short section of brass rod in place. This was then fitted to a pin vice so that I would not have to touch the tiny pieces whilst painting them.

The characters were primed and, in a break from my usual procedure when painting small figures, I airbrushed a base coat of each figure's main colour: Swedish Blue for *Penny* and Graveyard Earth for *Parker*. Having satisfied my masochistic tendencies for the month I decided not to shade the figures with the airbrush and went about this process using more traditional methods. I can understand why a lot of figure painters use oil colours as the slow drying time

allows for the blending of different shades to get a smooth transition that I would normally build on a larger scale figure with an airbrush. Not having any oil paints to hand, nor being quite ready to step out of that particular comfort zone, I kept to my traditional acrylic paints but added some *Liquitex Flow Retarder*: this slows down the drying time of the acrylic paint so that if you work in small sections at a time you will be able to achieve some limited blending. This has the advantage over oil colours as the retarded acrylics can still be quickly dried off with the application of heat from a hair dryer. To further help blend in the shadows I applied some pastel dust with a 1/8" chisel-tipped brush before giving each figure a coat of matt varnish to fix the pastels in place.

For the skin tones I used my usual mix of *Liquitex* Raw Sienna, Burnt Sienna and Titanium White, which was darkened with the addition of a little Burnt Sienna and Burnt Umber. The base flesh colour was lightened by adding increasing amounts of Unbleached Titanium White. On both figures I worked from dark to light and added some Red Oxide to the base flesh mix to act as a blusher for *Penny's* cheeks and give *Parker* his trademark red nose and jowls.

Penny's hair colour was created by mixing Yellow Oxide, Raw Sienna and Unbleached Titanium White. *Parker's* hair comes from a mix of Neutral Grey, Raw Umber and White. For

48: plastic tree armatures. 49: armatures bent and primed. 50: Raw Umber wash added. 51: Stone Grey wash applied.
52-53: grass sprinkled on and bushes glued in place. 54-55: dried pigments worked into road. 56: the completed base.

56

both figures the hair was given a flat base coat that was then accentuated by applying a series of washes and dry-brushes – alternating between the two to obtain a natural variation in shades without the powdery effect you can sometimes get from dry-brushing alone.

With the figures complete I came to position them in the car and realised that they would not fit without their feet being removed, a fact I would have been aware of if I had bothered to test fit them before assembly – lesson learned. *Penny* needs to be positioned as close to centre as possible if she is not to bang her head and prevent the canopy from fitting correctly. Trying to position the steering wheel in *Parker's* hands, seat *Parker* correctly and locate the wheel in its housing was a fiddly affair but, after a few good, stress-relieving swear words, *Parker* was ready to go. The canopy was then glued in place with *PVA* glue applied using the end of a cocktail stick.

For the base I masked off the edges of a wooden cutting board and gave it a coat of *Gesso* to prime it and to give me a plain surface on which to sketch out the proposed layout.

I had decided that I would like to introduce a substantial tree into the scene and selected a small oak tree from *Schleich's* range of scenery items. The tree is supplied as a main trunk with separate top branches and about twenty PVC foliage clusters. This particular tree stands about 250mm tall and its pre-painted finish would be perfectly adequate as a background scenery item. However, I wanted the tree to look a bit more realistic, so I set to work on it by supergluing the top branches to the trunk and applying some *Flexibark* over the join. As ever, the tree components had been thoroughly cleaned before working on them to remove any grease. *Flexibark* is a textured paste that is normally applied over wire-form trees to give them the appearance of tree bark. As the tree was already well textured I only needed to apply the product over the join and try to blend it in with the surrounding areas, although this was not super-critical as the foliage clusters hid most of the upper trunk. To prime the tree before painting I gave it a coat of *Gesso* mixed with some Dark Grey and Raw Umber paint so that I did not have a completely white base to work on. *Gesso* has the further advantage that, if applied thickly, it creates additional texture on the model.

To get a feel for the layout of the base I used the tree and car chassis to consider spatial relationships and allow me to mark out the dividing line between private and public land. With this line in place I test-fitted the gate to consider its location on the base, bearing in mind that I wanted the car to be mostly into the road for the diorama and considering *FAB 1*'s – presumably – large turning circle.

I prepared a road surface by taping cardboard strips to the perimeter of the designated area and also using the same thickness of cardboard to mask off positions for the road gully and manhole cover. I then trowelled on some *Liquitex Resin Gesso* that was smoothed off and levelled by scraping the surface with a straight edge and using the cardboard strips as the level edge. It may be necessary to apply a second coat locally to build up the levels, but a more realistic finish is obtained by the end result not being without flaws. The cardboard edging strips were removed and the entire area was painted with *Woodland Scenics* Asphalt Top Coat.

Sections of pavement were created by cutting out appropriate shapes using sheet balsa. These were then given a thin coating of *Foam Putty* to the top surface and some *Flexibark* to the edges. When dry these were sanded smoother and the paving slabs and edges were then carved into the sections using a riffling file. A stone plinth was created to the back of the pavement by using plastic sections from my spares box and filling their open ends with epoxy putty. The pavements were then coated with *Gesso* mixed with Raw Umber paint to give them both a primer and base colour in one.

To colour the pavements and stone plinth I roughly mixed Neutral Grey, Raw Umber, Yellow Oxide and Unbleached Titanium White on my palette. When I say 'rough mix' I mean that the colours were randomly mixed together and not fully blended. This left my palette with a mixture of different colours that were all in the correct tonal range. For the pavement I used a piece of torn sponge to randomly dab the colours to try and replicate the stone slabs. For the stone plinth I went down a slightly different route by first applying the colours in wash form then stippling them on with an old, stiff brush. By applying the same colours using different techniques I tried to produce a variance in texture between the two items yet still imply that they were both made from stone. Once the paint was dry I returned with distinct washes of Olive, Black and a mix of Raw Umber and Payne's Grey to emphasise the joints and suggest a little damp.

I wanted to paint the tree using washes to build up the colour and create a randomness that would not be possible otherwise. I used *Woodland Scenics'* range of liquid pigments, supplemented with *Liquitex* acrylic paints, all diluted with water. I started off by applying Yellow Ochre which, whilst still wet, was followed up with a coat of Raw Umber. The washes were applied randomly over the tree and then dried with a hair dryer so that I could immediately proceed with the next coat of Olive near the base of the tree. To tone the whole thing down I gave the tree an all-over wash of Stone Grey, which is a brown-grey with a hint of green. This was then warmed up by the application of a mixture of Raw and Burnt Umber. When dry I returned with some local application of more Olive and Stone Grey. The initial washes were very diluted but they became more viscous as I proceeded and wished to intensify the colours. The liquid pigments dry with a very matt finish, but the acrylics have a slight sheen to them so, when dry, I applied a coat of matt varnish to give the tree a consistent finish.

The vinyl foliage clusters are quite well finished, but I wanted to go for a slightly more realistic appearance. To do this I use *Noch's Scale Leaves*. These are incredibly small, individual pieces of paper cut out to resemble a leaf and come in a range of colours. I emptied a packet of olive coloured leaves into a plastic freezer bag, then each foliage cluster was coated with PVA glue, dropped into the bag and given a good shake to make sure it was fully coated. With so many clusters to store whilst they dried I pulled out an old roasting tin to keep them in. This was also useful for reclaiming any excess leaves that had fallen off during the drying process. Just make sure you give the tin a thorough clean before roasting spuds in it or you are likely to find an unwelcome garnish on your Sunday lunch.

I realised that this was the closest I was going to get to being a Percy Thrower (ask any UK resident over 50) and decided to create some small bushes for the borders. *Woodland Scenics* produce a series of bare plastic tree armatures that range in size from 3/4" to 7" and can be covered with various mock foliages. I used some of the smaller trees and bent the branches to suit. To make them look more realistic I went through the same painting process I had undertaken for the tree. For the foliage I used *WS's Fine Leaf Foliage*, which comes on 'branches' that can be used directly, or the foliage itself can be cut off for use with the armatures. I used a mixture of Medium, Light and Olive Green foliage that was pressed onto the armatures that had had *PVA* glue applied to the various sections of their branches. To 'fix' the foliage I sprayed the completed bushes with diluted *PVA* glue and set them to one side to dry.

I realised that the brass-etched gates and railing were too flimsy to stand on their own so decided to create some fence posts by using *Plastruct* I-sections cut to length. To make them a little more decorative I trimmed the tops off the posts at a 45-degree angle. I considered how to fix the fence to the posts and realised that in real life the fence panels would incorporate brackets, which would bolt to the posts. I went about creating a set of brackets by using the off-cuts of brass and bending them into 'L' shapes. These were then superglued onto the panels. I did not worry if there was a slight overspill of glue as it just looked like a welded joint when dry. The fence and gate panels were then primed and sprayed with gloss black. To add a little colour to the gates I used *Liquid Gold Leaf* to highlight various features.

Using *MiniArt's Park Accessories* kit I made up two lampposts and painted them satin black. Caution is the key word when handling the styrene in *MiniArt's* kits as it tends to be a little on the soft side. Generally there is no problem with this, except I wouldn't recommend the use of a hair

dryer to speed up the drying time of paint on these parts... unless you are trying to create an abstract sculpture. As a final move with these parts I subtly drybrushed the lampposts with Earth Brown to tone down the satin effect.

Returning to the baseboard I glued the stone plinths in place and gently bent some balsa strip to create the timber edges to the drive. These were painted with washes as described previously and the completed sections of pavement, along with the road gully and manhole cover, were glued to the board. Before laying the turf I wanted the tree fixed down so that it would look like it was growing out of the ground rather than just sitting on top of it. However, I did leave the foliage off until later so that my working space was not obstructed. The road gully and manhole cover were drybrushed with some dark red-browns to indicate a slight level of oxidation.

To create a layer of 'earth' I mixed up a batch of *Celluclay* with water, *PVA* glue and some Liquid Earth Pigment from *Woodland Scenics*. This was trowelled into place and worked around the roots of the tree so that its base was completely covered. The baseboard was then set aside for a couple of days to let the *Celluclay* dry out. I wanted to have an earth bed for planting that bordered the grassed areas and realised that this would need to be created before I laid the grass. In a clean herb jar I mixed together some fine cinders and earth scatter, both from *Woodland Scenics*, along with some *Fuller's Earth*. This mix gave me relative course, medium and fine textures for the earth, which would be coloured later. I spread some thinned PVA glue onto the borders and around the base of the tree, sprinkled the mix on and patted it down with my fingers. When this was dry I used *Mig* Russian Earth Pigment to colour the borders appropriately.

For the grass I was eager to try out my new toy – a *Noch Gras-Master*. For grassed areas in the past I had used various forms of scatter available from the Model Railway section of the local model shop, including static grass, which has a degree of length to the fibres but is usually laid flat. I had wondered for many years if there might be a way of getting the fibres to stand upright to replicate real blades of grass before recently discovering the *Gras-Master*. This device imparts a static charge onto the fibres so that, as they are sprinkled onto the pre-glued base they are attracted towards the *Gras-Master* but are held in place by the glue. Following the instructions I used some normal length static grass for the main areas and longer fibres next to the tree where it would be difficult to cut with a lawn mower. Whilst it may not be readily evident from the photographs the fibres mostly stood up, so I was pleased for a first attempt.

The drive was created by gluing fine Model Railway gravel in place in order to replicate a limestone path. The previously created bushes were glued in place with superglue, although some of the 'trunks' were cut short to make them look more like bushes than bonsai trees. I glued some dried herbs around the bases of the bushes, as well as around the pavements, to replicate deadfall. This was supplemented by some of the *Noch* leaves being sprinkled around the base of the tree and onto the drive.

To complete the base I wanted to add a layer of dust to the road and achieved this by using *Mig Pigments'* Dry and Dark Muds carried in enamel thinner. This was allowed to dry and the layer of dust loosened by rubbing the base with a stiff brush in the likely direction of traffic. With base and *FAB 1* complete it was time to bring them together and admire the view.

Daring-Do from Dan Dare's Dad
Creating a 1/48th alternate history spectacular

A s that great philosopher, *Hannibal Smith*, once said: 'I love it when a plan comes together,' and so do I, particularly as I work in the architectural profession. However, it can also be quite rewarding to consider the influences that have worked their way together, culminating in that 'eureka!' moment when all the mental images gel and you have a moment of inspiration that, in this instance, starts off a new modelling project. Unfortunately, these moments don't happen as frequently as I would like, and the vacancy for my muse is still open to all Charisma Carpenter look-a-likes (I'll accept Halle Berry types if push comes to shove).

I'm sure that if you are of a certain age, as am I, your early modelling career will have been influenced by which *Airfix* kits were available at your local newsagent. Once in the early 1970s I was able to get hold of the year's *Airfix* catalogue, and the range of kits was truly staggering compared to what I had seen to date. I remember being particularly impressed by the models and box art dioramas featuring World War II airfields. I tried to replicate them... and, by sticking a *Spitfire* kit and some plastic figures to a base made from an old cardboard box, failed miserably. Fortunately I persevered. I've always had a desire to create things, which was always encouraged by my parents, and that desire to recreate a scene in small scale has never left me... which, I suppose, is what led me to write this book.

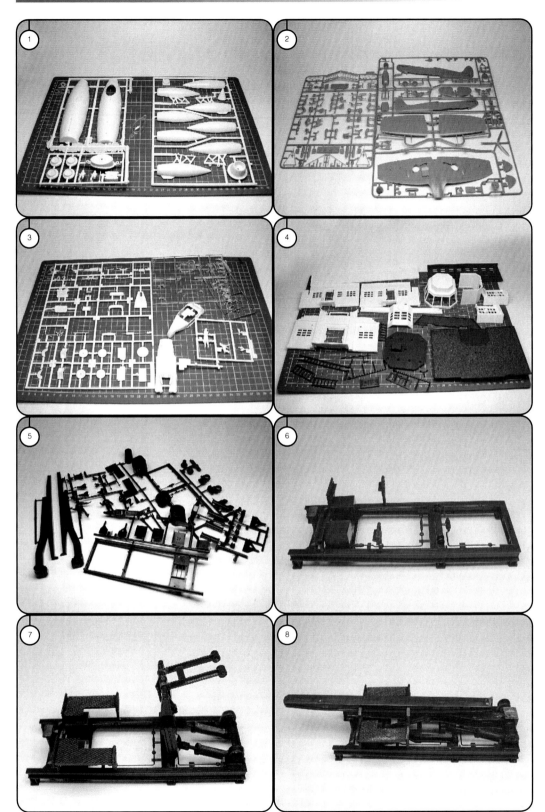

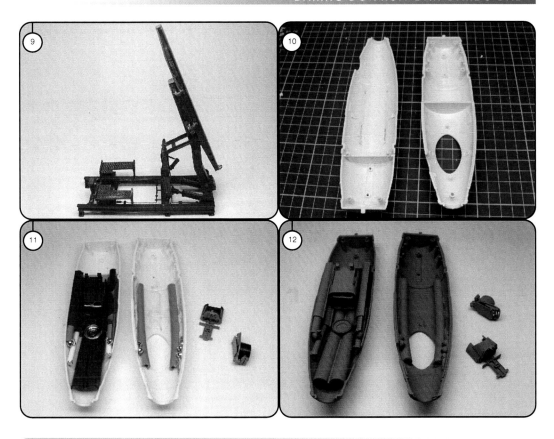

1- 5: combination of parts to create rocket, *Spitfire* and control tower. 6-9: launch platform. 10: rocket interior is scraped clear. 11: rocket interior parts assembled and fixed in place. 12: rocket interior primed.

Obviously as time passed a greater world of modelling opened out for me, with manufacturers fortunately finally realising that there was a market for Science Fiction and Fantasy kits amongst the tanks, planes and cars.

Model making aside, another of my interests is comic collecting, particularly those of the *Marvel* and *DC* variety. However, every self-respecting comic fan growing up in the 1970s also *had* to read the groundbreaking British comic *2000AD*. Whilst *Judge Dredd* (and no, I don't believe he's Welsh) was, and is, the star of the comic, it also made me aware of a character called *Dan Dare*, whom the publishers had revamped from his 1950s origins. Being a curious sort I wanted to know more about these original adventures, but at the time there were no reprint books about. A few years later I picked up a volume called *The Man from Nowhere* published by *Dragon's Dream*, which reprinted one of Frank Hampson's original *Dare* stories. The quality of the art and storytelling blew me away and I was fascinated by this hero, who stood for Truth, Justice and the English Way, and by the futuristic world he inhabited. That world was still influenced by an imperialistic England, but was one that focused on all the good aspects such as respect, fair play and doing the right thing. Fortunately, in the late 1980s and early 1990s, *Hawk Books* reprinted all of *Dan's* tales, which I highly recommend.

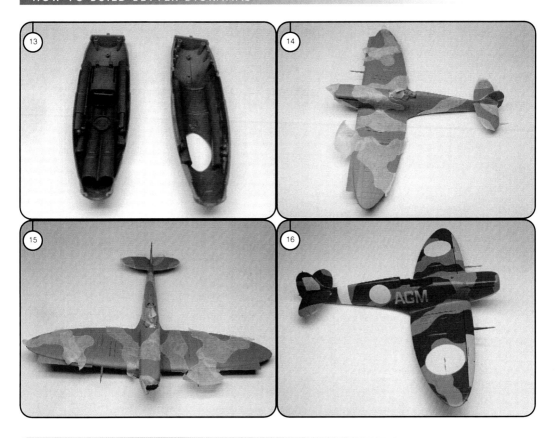

13: base coat applied to rocket interior. 14-15: *Spitfire* with base grey coat is masked. 16-17: yellow added to leading edge of wings whilst wings and fuselage are painted camouflage green. 18-19: decals applied. 20-22: cockpit detail. 23-24: completed interior.

In more recent years Warren Ellis and Chris Weston created a graphic novel called *The Ministry of Space* that looks at the history of space flight as it might have been if England had secured the services of the German rocket builders before the Americans and Russians, and only last year Garth Ennis and Gary Erskine brought *Dan Dare* out of retirement into a more cynical age to fight the good fight against a seemingly unstoppable menace.

The final pieces of the jigsaw of inspiration that resulted in this diorama came in the form of two kits, one being *Pegasus Hobbies' Apollo 27* spaceship and the other a 1940s *BMW* car I found when browsing a website. I was quite intrigued by the design of the *Apollo 27*, but felt that it had a more 'retro' than futuristic feel, and that with a few more rivets it could have almost passed for *Wallace and Gromit's* rocket in **A Grand Day Out**. The car kit came with a figure of a woman and a dog, and reminded me of someone driving up to an airfield to wave good-bye to her husband as he sets out on a mission during World War II.

Somehow all these pieces came together in my head to create a scenario. What if Germany had been more successful in rocket technology and had developed manned rockets, not to travel to the stars, but as a new form of fighting machine? Necessity being the mother of invention, the *Royal*

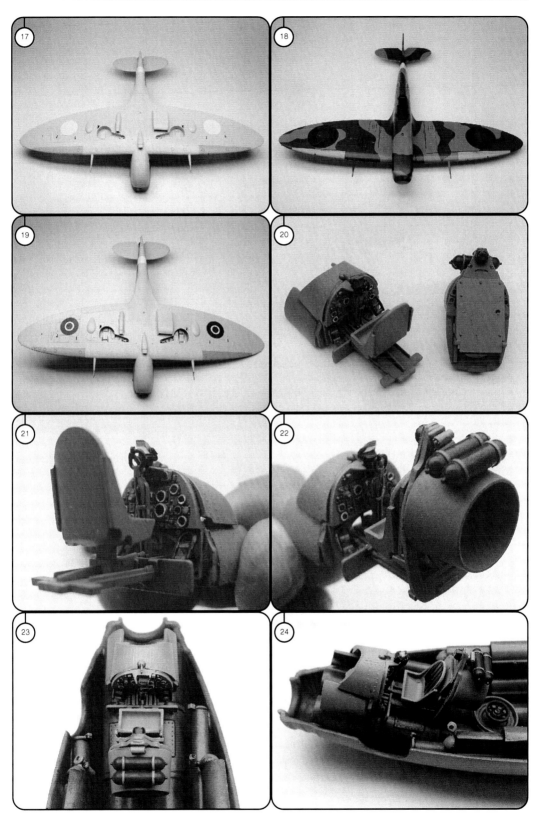

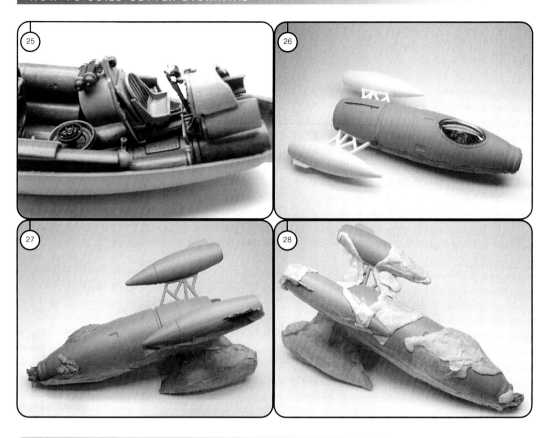

25: completed interior. 26: rocket fuselage ready for sanding. Opposite inset: base coat and masking. 27: second coat of French Blue Grey applied to fuselage of model. 28: camouflage masking is added.

Air Force would develop their own form of rocket fighters to defend England from attack. As part of the official *Dare* history, *Dan Dare's* Dad had disappeared whilst being employed as a test pilot, so the lady supplied with the car could be *Jean Dare*, coming to wave her husband *William* off on a mission he would not return from.

In addition to the *Apollo 27* and *BMW 327* (yes, I know it's German, but I couldn't find any other kit of a car of the period in 1:48 scale) I purchased *Tamiya's Supermarine Spitfire Mk.Vb* to add to the feel that the rockets were a developing technology during war time and more traditional forms of flight were more commonly in use. This kit was also very useful as it came with a set of seven crew figures. An 0-scale airport from *Bachmann* was also selected, as 0-scale works out at 1:43, which was close enough to 1:48 to not look out of proportion, and the kit in question appears to be Art Deco in design, which suited the period nicely. Rounding out the collection of kits are two *Revell Nike Hercules* missiles, which had just been re-released and featured a really nice launch platform that could be adjusted to suit the *Apollo 27*.

If you'll bear with me for a moment or two I'll just climb onto my soapbox. I don't often buy military kits and I was very impressed with the level of detail that came with the ones I bought –

a level of detail that puts most commercially available SF&F kits to shame. Even the fifty-year-old *Nike Hercules* kit is well detailed and includes figures to give the model scale – things that SF&F kit manufacturers should take note of if this sector of the modelling hobby is to be taken more seriously by the model-making hobby as a whole. Whilst I appreciate that we are seen as more of a niche market and therefore kits are going to be more expensive because they are only produced in limited numbers, there is no comparison between the quality and number of parts in the *Tamiya Spitfire* kit compared to the *Pegasus Apollo 27*. End of sermon – back to your regular programme.

I decided to start my kit-building programme with the models that would need the least modification: the *Spitfire* and the two launch platforms. Examining the *Spitfire* kit I found that it had a wonderfully detailed cockpit that could be used in the rocket. Obviously this meant that the *Spitfire* would be missing this detail, but as it was intended to be a background element, and not that much of the cockpit is visible once assembled, I felt justified in borrowing it – besides, I had ideas of how to hide the fact that there would be no internal detail in the aircraft.

Now before I begin describing my construction work on the aircraft please bear in mind that the last time I built a *Spitfire* would have been around 1974, or even earlier, and I don't have any great interest in military or aircraft modelling. I may therefore take liberties in the way that the model is built and painted that I feel I can justify as this scene belongs to an 'alternative history', but at no time do I mean any disrespect to the valiant pilots and crew who fought to ensure that we had a better future.

For the most part I followed the *Spitfire* kit's instructions, obviously omitting the section on the cockpit build up. Once I had the two fuselage halves joined and the wings added I decided to carry out the bulk of the painting, as I did not want to start applying the tiny detail pieces too soon as these were obvious 'targets' that could easily be knocked off as I handled the plane. I chose to more or less follow the colour scheme described in the instructions but to substitute my own colour choices. So, after priming the kit and stuffing tissue paper into the cockpit to mask the coat of Olive I had sprayed in there, I gave the model a base coat of *Liquitex* French Blue Grey. Not being sure whether the camouflaging should have a hard or a soft edge I decided to use masking tape cut with an irregular edge to give a firm definition between the two colours. A coat of *Games Workshop*'s Catachan Green was airbrushed on to complete the camouflage patterning. The instructions described the underside colour as 'sky' so I chose a very pale blue–grey mix that I had originally made up to paint the *USS Enterprise* comprising Titanium White, Neutral Grey and French Blue Grey. This definitely needed a

29: basic board layout is marked out. 30: section of board removed to accept cobbles. 31: concrete laid. 32: cobble stones laid. 33: first of the colour washes added to control tower. 34: colour of tower is built up with a second wash colour.

hard edge to the previously painted camouflage, but I thought that, as the colour was going to be applied on the opposite side to the previous paintwork, the body of the plane would act as its own mask as long as I was careful with the angle I held the airbrush at, so I only masked along the edge and not the rest of the fuselage. Big mistake. Rather than use the fine tip in my airbrush I kept in the high flow tip, which is ideal for spraying large, plain areas. Unfortunately, the high flow was very high and the amount of overspray was far greater than expected, which meant that the sides of the plane now featured a pale grey mist over the camouflaged areas. With all the masking removed I went back to the kit with a brush to touch up the flawed areas. By keeping the paint fluid and carefully working in to minimise brush strokes, I was able to create a satisfactory finish, which was further improved with a coat of matt varnish. The fuselage was then given a coat of gloss varnish in preparation for the application of the decals.

Whilst the varnish dried I went back to the sprues and painted all the small parts before removing them so that I had something to hold onto. Unusually the decals came as a two-part application with white circles to act as backings for the coloured roundels for the wings and fuselage, so I decided to make the decal application a two-stage procedure to hopefully minimise handling problems. The white circles and other markings were positioned in the normal manner

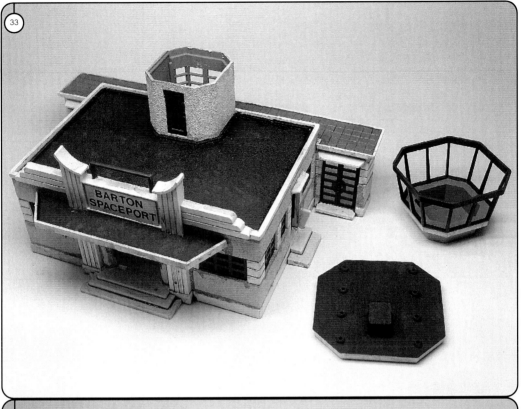

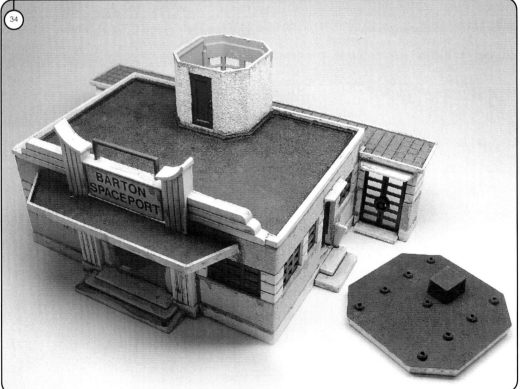

using the two-part decal setting solutions *Micro Sol* and *Micro Set*, applied to the surface of the model before and after decal application appropriately. The two large circles to the upper surface of the wings needed a slit cutting into them with a sharp scalpel blade so that they would conform around a surface blip before the application of the *Micro Set*. Once the decals had dried they were given a coat of varnish prior to the application of the coloured roundels, as I did not want the water on the roundels to loosen the white circles beneath. The procedure was then repeated for the coloured roundels, but when I came to examine the model after the third coat of varnish had dried I noticed that, whilst all the decals were securely in place, the top wing roundels looked decidedly wrinkled on close inspection. I don't know why this happened, as none of the other decals were similarly affected, but it just goes to show that even with the best laid plans things can go awry. Anyway, no use worrying – the defect is only noticeable on close inspection and I've already stated that the *Spitfire* is intended to be a background item and not a prominent part of the diorama. Besides, there are lots more things in our lives more important than a modelling project that doesn't quite go to plan, so it's always good to keep these things in perspective.

I next gave the *Spitfire* a coat of matt varnish as it would more readily accept further paintwork than the gloss finish, so that I could commence weathering prior to adding the detail items to the kit I had been concerned would break off if installed too soon in the construction process. I had been made aware of the *Tensocrom* range of weathering paints manufactured by *Lifecolor* and decided to give it them a try. These come with descriptions such as Oil, Smoke, Rust, etc. and are low-viscosity, translucent acrylics. The translucency allows the paints to be layered on top of each other to create different effects, and the paint is thin enough to run into all the nooks and crannies without the need for thinning. I felt that the most appropriate colours to use would be Smoke (black) and Oil (a dark brown) and found them to be

35-36: two views of the completed control tower. Inset: the completed rocket.

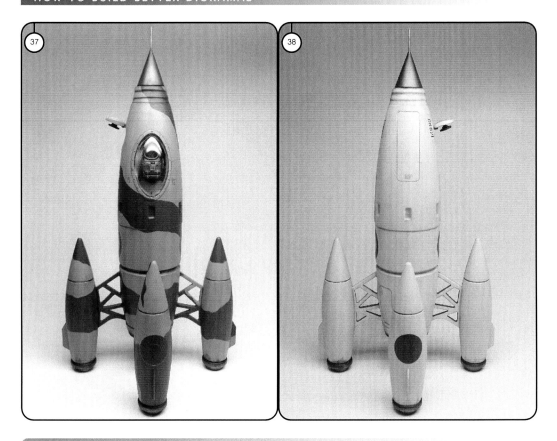

37-38: top and underside views of the completed rocket. 39: cockpit detail showing blister treated with *Johnson's Klear.*

most useful in creating subtle weathering effects. They ran nicely into the many fine recessed panel lines on the kits and any over-run was easily wiped off with my finger.

I masked off the clear sections of the canopy so that I could paint the panel lines in colours to match the fuselage and glued the completed parts in place with a clear-drying PVA glue. Whilst most of the interior is obscured by the canopy it was still noticeably empty, so now it was time to bring in my secret weapon – a coat of matt varnish. The kit needed a final coat of varnish to give it an even finish and fix any pigment powders anyway, but the varnish, sprayed over the clear parts, gave them a misted-over finish obscuring the lack of internal detail. As part of the diorama we can justify this obscure canopy as early morning frost, condensation, or just the need for a darn good clean.

I decided to build the launch platforms straight from the box and, once complete, I would build some form of suspension between them to hold the rocket. Looking at the instructions they recommended that most of the parts be painted Olive, which seemed as good a paint scheme as any, considering the subject matter. Whilst many of the detail parts needed accent colours I decided to build both platforms and then airbrush them Olive, as the fact that a lot of the parts are push-fitted together so that the platforms can be raised meant that the components could be

disassembled to paint any detail areas. For a kit with fifty-year-old moulds the parts are really well detailed, although the seam lines are quite significant and there is some flash to be removed. Once assembled both platforms worked as they should, although one of them had a slight twist in it that would straighten with the application of heat, and this would not prove to be a problem in any case as I intended to glue both platforms down to a base once I had completed the paintwork.

I dismantled the launch platforms and began the detail painting that pretty much followed the suggestions in the instructions – as the model is mostly Olive this did not take too long to complete – so that I could then give some consideration as to how the launch platforms would support the rocket.

My initial thoughts for resting the rocket on the platforms was to create some kind of cradle that would span between the raised rails of the platform, but I had to discount this because of the bottom engine of the rocket. This being the case I realised I would need some kind of rail either side of the rocket's main hull to keep the gap in between clear. To help with some hands-on trial and error I set the platform's top rail at an angle of approximately thirty degrees and glued all the joints in position to create a rigid structure to build off. I simply butted the two platforms together but the gap between the top rails was too wide to support the rocket and, whilst I could have carried out some surgery on the platforms to bring them closer together, I decided that I wanted to have a slightly more elaborate top rail design. Now, as all self-respecting SF modellers know, there is only one port of call when it comes to girder- and rail- type structures: the *Airfix* (now *Dapol*) *Girder Bridge* kit. Extensively used by Derek Meddings and the *Century 21* model department, the kit is a great source of parts for scratchbuilding and kit-bashing. Playing about with the parts I chose a couple of girder rails and the top bracing parts cut in half as supports. After some test-fitting with *Blu-Tac* as a temporary fix I glued the parts together before giving them a quick coat of black primer then painting them in Boltgun Metal to match the rails of the platforms. The two platforms were then varnished and decals applied ready for weathering.

I turned my attention to the rocket and, after some initial test-fitting, it became obvious that, although not marketed as such, the kit could be considered as a push-fit with glue an optional extra. The four side rockets were glued together and a little filler was applied to the join line. The supplied cockpit detail was abandoned to accommodate the larger scale detailing I wished to add. This meant that the inside of the two hull halves would be visible through the large canopy and through the hatch, which I wanted to model in an open position. Therefore, I was going to have

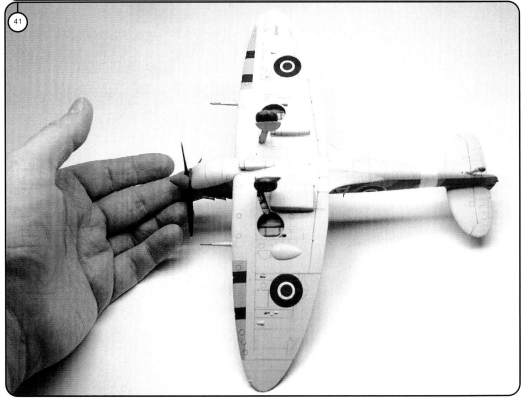

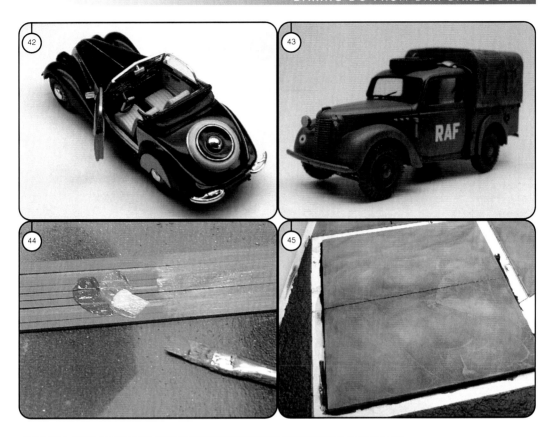

40-41: the completed 1/48th scale *Spitfire*. 42: appropriate car for the scale and period. 43: RAF truck.
44: painting kerb edgings. 45: concrete plinth and planting beds.

to do a little more detailing than I had initially thought and the first task to accomplish was the removal of all the large locating lugs on the inside so that any detailing could sit flat against the hull. I used a pair of clippers to snap off the worst of the lugs then went in with a sanding drum in my power tool to smooth the inside. The inevitable burr produced by using a power tool on styrene-type plastic was removed with a quick once over with a flexible sanding pad, available from the painting section of your local DIY shop and highly recommended.

I was considering what wiggits I could use from the spares box to decorate the interior when my gaze settled on the missile components of the *Nike Hercules* kits and I realised that the cylindrical sections would make an ideal lining for the rocket. Once glued in place not only did they look right but I could justify the design as internal fuel tanks, as there is not a lot of engine room in the design, which further added to the high risk nature of test piloting such a craft. Further detailing was added using some plastic cylinder and channel section (thanks to Des and Steve at the *Manchester Modelzone* for helping out with a few kit-bashed parts to complete the lining). These changes to the kit meant that the canopy had to be adjusted to now fit in place and the hatch had to be cut down to remove its square support. I test-fitted the *Spitfire* cockpit parts in the rocket and realised that the cockpit frame would need to be extended to the front and rear to cover the ends of the frame that were never meant to be on show. Once again parts from the missile kit came in useful after being cut to fit and suit the new arrangement of the cockpit. I left the cockpit frame in two halves to make detail painting easier and sprayed it French Blue Grey and the inside of the hull Olive.

Whilst most of the interior would be obscured I wanted it to be detailed enough for inspection through the canopy and open hatch. I gave the whole of the inside of the hull a heavy wash with thinned black paint and allowed it to dry. I did this to emphasise all the recesses and detail, but swiftly remembered that you should never model when feeling tired as you'll regret it the morning after when you review the results. The application of black was far too haphazard and needed tidying up by first going back with a brush coat of Olive paint. As the paint is slightly translucent a lot of the black was not fully obscured and I also wanted to add a secondary colour to the paint scheme. To this end I brush painted some Raw Umber into recesses and pipe joints to give the appearance of wear and spills. Whilst I appreciate that this craft is meant to be fairly new I justified this approach by reasoning that in wartime there would be a shortage of materials and some of the internal parts had therefore been cannibalised from earlier prototypes or crashed vehicles. To tone down the colour variation I gave the interior a further brush coat of Olive then added some accent colours to the wiggets. After learning my lessons, I gave the cockpit frame a careful pin wash with the *Tensocrom* Smoke and Oil and completed the detail painting of the components before gluing the frame in place.

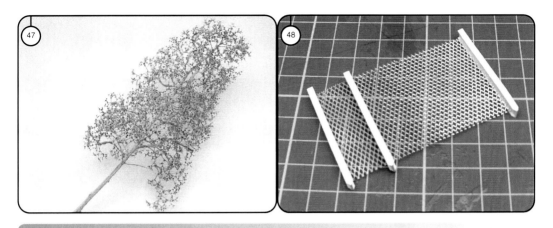

46: rocket launcher in situ. 47: sea moss. 48: miniature fence under construction.

I followed the instructions and placed the two side rockets on their locating lugs and joined the two halves together. With the removal of the locating lugs the halves of the hull kept wanting to twist relative to each other and the usual technique of applying liquid cement using capillary action was not securing them together quickly enough to prevent distortion. The circular section of the craft meant that clamping the parts together would not be easy and rubber bands would not have sufficient strength to hold the parts whilst the glue dried, so, section by section, I ran superglue into the join and hit it with an accelerator to set it instantly and strengthen the joint. I then went back with liquid cement and applied it generously to try and weld the halves together.

It was during this glue application that I had another 'Oh, b****r!' moment: some of the liquid cement had run and streaked onto the canopy. Whilst I could have bought another kit to obtain a new canopy I objected to the additional expense and with deadlines for completing the book looming I could not afford the downtime in a trip to the shops and back tracking on the work completed to date. Knowing that *Dettol Multi-Surface Cleaner* is very good at removing paint I soaked the end of a cotton bud with some of the cleaner and gently rubbed the surface of the canopy. I kept repeating this process with a degree of success but the stain was still noticeable, so I considered further options and was tempted to create some canopy framing to hide it, but was reticent to go down this route as it would further obscure the view into the cockpit. I then remembered reading that many modellers coat their clear parts with *Johnson's Klear* floor polish to improve their appearance, so I decided to give it a try, as I could always fall back on the canopy framing if it did not work. And I am very pleased to report that, after brushing on a coat of the *Klear*, not only did the canopy look nice and shiny, but the stain had all but disappeared. Deep sigh of relief.

With the panic over I filled and sanded the join between the halves and regretted inserting the two engines as per the instructions as they only got in the way. Once I was satisfied with the join I affixed the top and bottom engines and masked off the canopy and open areas prior to giving the model a coat of spray primer. I left off the engine caps and nose cone for ease of painting.

I wanted the rocket to have the same paint scheme as the *Spitfire* but approached it differently to apply the lessons learned from painting the aircraft. I airbrushed my Sky Blue mix to the bottom half of the rocket then fully masked it off to avoid any problems with overspray. The top half was then given two coats of French Blue Grey. Rather than using masking tape for the camouflaging I cut thin strips of *Blu-Tac* then applied them to the model in a pattern similar to the *Spitfire*. The areas between the *Blu-Tac* were covered with masking tape and I found this to be much easier than the method I had used on the aircraft. I used a fresh pack of *Blu-Tac* to get the thin strips but it is possible to re-use old *Blu-Tac* by running it through a pasta machine to squeeze it into thin, flat strips – just don't use the pasta machine afterwards for food preparation! With the masking complete I airbrushed two coats of Catachan Green to complete the camouflage pattern. All remaining parts were sprayed a 50-50 mixture of *Games Workshop*'s Boltgun Metal and Black.

With the paintwork complete I repeated the same process for the markings as per the *Spitfire*, using left over markings from the *Spitfire* kit and a 1:35 scale model of a *Tiger Moth* I had build as *Thunderbird 6* (Pick up a copy of *Sci.Fi & Fantasy Modeller – Modelling the 21st. Century Volume 2* for more details – and a darn good read.). Because the rocket was lacking in panel detailing I set about adding panel lines using a 2B graphite pencil and masking tape as a guide. Weathering was added by smudging the graphite with a moist finger and by using *Mig* Black Pigment Powder. Before giving the whole lot a further coat of matt varnish to fix the powder and graphite I examined the rocket from all angles as it is very easy for the Pigment Powder to go where you don't want it to, but equally easy to wipe off using a damp tissue.

I removed all the masking tape and gave the canopy another coat of *Klear*, but realised that there was a marking on the inside that I was just going to have to live with. To complete the rocket I glued a 1:72 tank wheel to the inside of the hatch and used a couple of small parts from the *Spitfire* kit's figure sprue as the hinges.

The car was built and painted next and I pretty much just followed the instructions to complete it. There are, however, a few points worth noting about the paintwork. The car needed a high gloss finish and I first considered using gloss paints to obtain this but decided on another route for a couple of reasons. The car has a two-tone colour scheme and the cream colour I wanted to use is not available in a gloss finish. Even if I had been able to obtain the paint, gloss is best sprayed rather than brush applied and, because of the small size of the car and the complex colour pattern masking between colours, would have been extremely difficult to brush paint on. To paint the car I therefore airbrushed a coat of *Liquitex* Unbleached Titanium White as a base colour then brush painted the Black by using two thin coats rather than one thick one to minimise the appearance of brush strokes. Before I applied the detail parts to the model I masked off the interior and sprayed three heavy coats of gloss varnish to give the car a nice sheen. Once the varnish was thoroughly dry I went back to the instructions and completed the application and painting of the detail parts, some of which I have to say are extremely small and careful breath

49: upper rear view of completed launcher. 50: completed tree. 51-54: 1/48th scale figures.

control needs to be observed if you don't want them to disappear into that well known black hole called the carpet. The car was completed with a little drybrushing of Raw Sienna and Earth Brown to the underside and wheel arches to simulate mud splatter.

The airport was built straight from the box, although the tower was left off until later so that it could be glazed and detail added once the overall painting had been completed. The join at the corners was poor and needed filling, although I did not worry particularly about the finish as I had plans for the surface of the building. Speaking of the surface, I could not believe that, over the main doors in embossed lettering, was the legend *Plasticville Airport* – bang goes any element of reality. Never mind, I could overboard these with a more appropriate sign... as *Dan Dare* comes from Manchester I decided that the building would become *Barton Spaceport*. By the way, the next time some 220lb muscle-bound beach bum kicks sand in your model making face there's no need to turn to Charles Atlas for help – you can simply remind this bully that one of *Dan Dare's* hobbies is model making and you'll see his scorn turn to immediate admiration. ...I think I'll lie down now, my imagination is beginning to scare me.

I scraped off the lettering with a small chisel and the building was primed. I started the painting by spraying all the doors and windows *Liquitex* Hooker's Green (and, no, I don't why it's called Hooker's Green). These were masked off and I sprayed the remainder of the building white, as this would become my base colour for the painted concrete areas. The reason why I was not too concerned about the finish to the joints was because I intended the walls to be finished to replicate textured render. I set about this by base coating the main wall sections with *Liquitex* Unbleached Titanium White, as I realised that such a pale colour would need to be built up in layers. To create my textured surface I took some of the base colour and thinned it with a little water, mixing in some talcum powder and a little *Resin Stucco* to help bind the mixture. I then applied the mixture, which needed two coats to achieve the desired colour and texture, with a dabbing technique using a stiff, flat ended, stencilling brush.

The roofs were base coated black and then, to give them a slight texture, I added some black to my left over wall texture (by the way, this will keep for a good while if you cover it with cling film and store it in the fridge). This created a very dark grey paste that was applied with a sponge to leave a slight texture, but not as pronounced as that on the walls. I then tidied up any over-spills before starting the weathering.

One of the advantages of using artist's acrylics is that many of them are slightly translucent when applied as a single coat – this enables us to build up the final colour using layers of colour to achieve variations that can then be brought together at the end with a final layer of the base colour. Using the intermediate colours thinned, or as washes, also helps with the tonal variations. I started off by using a Raw Umber wash in all the recesses and areas where water would collect or drip, such as the edges of windowsills. Payne's Grey was added to the wash to emphasise these areas, but applied with more restraint than the initial wash. The base colours were then drybrushed over the washed areas, using quite a 'wet' brush, to blend everything together and reduce any over spill of the washes.

With all the paintwork complete I set about glazing the building using clear *plasticard*. Because of the design of the kit I was able to tape most of the *plasticard* in place with *Scotch Invisible Tape* and only the tower and doors needed clear-drying PVA glue to fix the glazing in position. Not wanting to build an interior for the model that would be hardly seen when complete I cut some matt black card to size and formed an 'X' shape with two pieces of card slit together. This was then inserted into the building to create a sense of depth behind the windows without letting light through the tower to show its emptiness.

Before starting work on the kits I had realised that the base would have to be of a reasonable size and chose to use 5mm *foamboard* as none of the models were of any great weight. Prior to construction I had laid the parts out on an A1 sheet of *foamboard* to get a rough arrangement of parts and realised that I could fit everything onto an A2 sized sheet. To this end I cut the A1 sheet in half and glued the two pieces together with PVA glue to produce a more rigid board. When doing this I would recommend weighing down the boards to stop any movement or warping. One of the down sides of using *foamboard* is that the edge is both unattractive and prone to damage, so I decided to apply a rigid edging strip to resolve both issues. I had intended to use some 10mm plastic angle sections from my local DIY shop, but when I got there I found that they had none in stock. As an aside, have you ever noticed that large DIY shops never have exactly what you want? You go in to buy four white shelf brackets and they only have three, so you end up buying four grey ones or four white ones from the more expensive range! So, with no angle sections available I searched the racks for an alternative, came across some 10mm channel sections and decided to give them a go – if they wouldn't fit over the edges of the board I could always cut off one of the flanges to make some angle sections. Fortunately the channels did fit so I mitred the ends to frame the *foamboard* and glued the edges together with a little superglue.

As well as the figures that came with the *Spitfire* I bought a separate set of *RAF Personnel* to help populate the scene. Unfortunately, when the kits arrived in the post I found that the figures with the *Spitfire* were a duplicate of the separate set, even though they came from a different manufacturer. One of the down sides of ordering over the Internet is that you can't open the box before buying – never mind, though, as, with a little limb swapping and surgery, I was able to create some suitable, differently posed figures, although the personnel do appear to have been cloned if you look too closely. The figures fitted together very well and only needed a minimum of filling at the joints with two-part epoxy putty before priming in white.

I decided to use a batch painting technique for the figures as most of them would be painted using the same colours. This means, for example, painting the flesh on one figure and then the flesh on the next and so on, rather than painting all the colours on one figure at a time. This has the advantage that once you have finished painting the last figure the paint will be dry on the first and the process is more time efficient with more economic pant usage because you are only using one colour at a time. I began by giving all the flesh areas a coat of my standard flesh mix of Raw Sienna, Burnt Sienna and White. The flesh was then given a wash using *Games Workshop*'s Sepia and highlighted with some lightened flesh tones. A mistake would be to make the eyes a brilliant white, as they are not this colour naturally, but especially so at this small scale, so I added some Titanium White to my base flesh and broke out the 5/0 and 10/0 to apply the paint. When painting such small areas it is vitally important to have the paint fluid enough that it naturally flows off the brush, but not too thin that it swamps the model when applied. A steady hand and a good squint to help the old eyesight also won't do any harm. With a not-quite-black made from Raw Umber and Payne's Grey the pupils were dotted and a horizontal line added as combined upper eye-lash and shading. The hair was painted with various shades of brown, and blond hair was created using a mix of Raw Sienna, Yellow Oxide and Unbleached Titanium White.

Turning my attention to painting the uniforms I decided against going for traditional *RAF* colours and to base the uniforms on the *Spacefleet* green seen in the *Dan Dare* strip. I chose *Vallejo* Medium Olive as the base colour, as it has just enough of an olive hint to the green to look more military than grass. I mixed up a darker wash colour by adding Raw Umber and just a hint of black to the Olive and gave the clothed areas of the figures an overall wash with this colour. With the wash dry I went back with the base colour and applied it to the raised areas. This was then further highlighted by adding Unbleached Titanium White to the Medium Olive and applying the paint to edges of creases, collars, etcetera.

I won't go into every detail of painting the rest of the clothes – suffice it to say that I followed the same procedure of base colour followed by wash followed by base colour and finished with highlight. Most of the remaining clothes were leather goods – shoes, belts, jackets – and were painted with various shades of brown. The figure set was accompanied by two dogs, and, whilst it is a great shame that the model manufacturer did not take the opportunity to sculpt that most magnificent of breeds, the Cairn Terrier (Hello, Hattie), it is worth commenting on the painting technique I used to finish these canines. Each was given a base colour of brown, this being followed by a slightly darker, transparent brown. This second coat was applied in stokes that followed the direction of the dog's coat and, when dry, was repeated, but only to the recessed areas where shadowing needed to be applied. At such a small scale as this we are not trying to show individual hairs but rather imply that the surface is textured and not a flat colour.

One final point when painting such small figures: remember to take short breaks to try and minimise eye strain and tiredness, and remember your eyes take longer to change focal distance the older you get.

With the component models completed I started laying out the board formally in preparation for the application of the landscaping materials. When designing a diorama like this you have to give some consideration to 'compressing' reality to keep the scene visually interesting and to a manageable size. In reality you are not going to build a rocket launch pad next to an airport building, but if I were to build the diorama with a more realistic gap between them I would be constructing large areas of bare concrete or other ground finish. Not only would this be visually boring, but the base board could not be easily stored or displayed, so the overriding consideration has to be given to telling a story in three dimensions rather than strict scale modelling.

Onto the *foamboard* I sketched out my final layout, giving thought to what the landscape finishes would be. Whilst the rocket launcher would be mounted on a raised concrete plinth I felt that there should be an adjacent concrete area to serve the more traditional aircraft and so decided to start work on that first. I had already marked out the concrete yard area but this would need movement joints adding to create approximately 6m square bays. I marked these out then covered

the joint lines with thin strips of masking tape. I then lined the perimeter of the concrete area with strips of scrap cardboard of an equivalent thickness to the plastic edge strips. To create the concrete texture I mixed up a batch of *Liquitex Resin Stucco* and *Gesso*, which I pre-coloured using a mixture of Raw Umber and Neutral Grey paint. I added the *Gesso* to the *Resin Stucco* to try and reduce the texturing effect, which would not be as noticeable at the small scale of this diorama. The mixture was applied to the base with a small trowel and then levelled off by scraping across the top with the flat edge of an old plastic ruler – the cardboard strips provided me with a guide to run the ruler across to keep a consistent thickness to the mixture. The base was then set aside for twenty-four hours to thoroughly dry before the next stage, then set aside for a further twenty-four hours when my finger went into a soft spot causing some patch repairs that would be later sanded down to get an even finish across the area of concrete. When thoroughly dry the masking tape was removed to reveal the joints in the concrete and the cardboard edge strips were disposed of. Some of the concrete mix had dried on the plastic edge strips, but this was quickly sanded off.

To create the concrete plinth I cut a section of *foamboard* to size and added a single strip of masking tape down the middle. Another batch of 'concrete' paste was mixed up, but I went for a slight colour variation as the concrete for this and the airstrip would most likely have come from separate batches in reality, and the concrete would wear differently because of its different use and being raised above the ground level. To create this colour mix I used *Woodland Scenics* Concrete, Raw Umber and a hint of Slate Grey. I did not use the Concrete as supplied as it is a little too yellow in colour for my liking. Once dry the masking tape was removed and the plinth was glued down to the base with PVA and weighted down until the glue set.

To weather the concrete I applied washes of Raw Umber then darkened this with Payne's Grey. The washes were blended by rubbing the surface with my finger tip. A thinned black paint was run into the gaps between concrete panels and any over spill was also blended in with my finger. To try and tie all the colours together I created another wash using Neutral Grey, Raw Umber and Unbleached Titanium White and applied it in a similar manner to the other washes.

I had decided to try a different technique for the cobbled street in front of the Spaceport and purchased a box of 1:48 cobblestones from *Plus Models*. To accommodate the thickness of these 'stones' I carefully cut out the top sheet of *foamboard* from the base in the area where I wanted the road to be. Because of the uneven shape of the stones it would be very difficult to just glue them in place and get anything like a level finish so I chose to bed the stones in 'mortar', which in this instance was *Polyfilla Fine Surface Filler*. I applied the filler, using an artist's palette knife as a trowel, to a small section of the work area so that it did not start drying out before the stones were laid. The stones were simply pushed into the filler, keeping the top surface roughly level, and any filler that squeezed out between them was wiped off, leaving the gap between stones filled. With all the stones laid I realised the surface needed a good clean to remove the excess filler I had missed as I went along, so I wiped over the top with a damp sponge, as you would when removing grout from tiles. Unfortunately I forgot that the stones had been cast from a plaster type material that dissolved to create an almost uniform surface, so I let the stones and filler dry and gave the surface a quick sand to find that the surface was quite acceptable and ready for the application of weathering.

With hindsight I should have pre-coloured the *Polyfilla* to create a natural mortar finish between the cobbles, but felt that I could get rid of the off white colour by using my old stand-by technique of brushing on – wiping off *Liquitex Woodstain*. Unfortunately, all I ended up with was darkened stones, because they had absorbed the liquid from the stain, and the *Polyfilla* remained stubbornly white. Looking at the result I realised that many of the cobbles had blended together too well and any washes or other weathering techniques would not show the gaps between the stones so I was going to have to paint all the cobbles individually.

I based the cobbled area with a mixture of Raw Sienna, Raw Umber and Neutral Grey. I varied the mix of this base colour and sponged on the results to try and create tonal variations. Mixing Black and Raw Umber together to get a very dark grey I went about outlining each cobble stone. I thinned the paint slightly to help the flow and so that it would flow into any of the remaining recesses. I then created washes using lightened variations of the base colour and randomly applied the paint to try and further give the impression that the area was made up of individual stones and not one homogeneous mass.

I realised that each of the surface areas would need edging and I decided to use 1.5 x 2mm plastic strips, rather than cutting strips from *plasticard*, to ensure continuity of size. To help cut down on painting time I bundled all the strips together and held them in place with a bulldog clip. After priming the bundle I laid it flat on some scrap card and applied spots of three paints: Raw Sienna, Neutral Grey and Unbleached Titanium White. These were then blended together on the plastic strips to create natural colour variations and streaks. Each side was dried with a hair dryer before turning over and repeating the process, enabling the strips to be painted much more rapidly

than doing them one at a time. When dry the strips were then cut into 30mm lengths to represent 1200mm long edging strips and glued into place on the baseboard.

To try and make life easier I thought I would use textured *plasticard* to represent the paving slabs rather than cutting them out individually. Unfortunately I could find neither the right size nor pattern commercially, so I created my own using some plain *plasticard* and a *Tamiya* scribing tool. I drafted a paving layout on the *plasticard* and lined up the scribing tool with a steel rule, as you would do to cut with a knife, then drew the scriber backward along the rule to create a groove in the plastic. Once the pattern was complete I rubbed over the *plasticard* with a sanding pad to remove any remaining burrs. The paving was then painted using the same technique as the plastic strips, but using a sponge to mix/apply the paint. The grooves were then accentuated using a pin wash left over from lining the cobblestones.

I had glued the building to the base before cutting and gluing the paving slabs as I wanted it to look more sat-in rather than sat-on for a more realistic appearance. Although I had used the building as a template before fixing it in place there were still some slight gaps in some places between the building and the paving that needed filling realistically. To do this I created a 'mortar' from plaster, diluted PVA glue and some buff coloured pigment powder. This was trowelled in place and any excess wiped off with a moistened paper towel.

For the gravel path I had to use a very fine gravel, in reality probably a very course sand, as the particle sizes had to look realistic next to the figures' feet. The best way of gauging this is to hold a figure next to your selected gravel and compare the size of the figure's foot to the gravel to get an idea of if you're on the right track. Model Railway ballast is a good source for this. The gravel areas were painted with PVA glue and the gravel was sprinkled over. The previously placed edgings

created a good barrier for over spill. Whilst the gravel was still wet I ran the car through it to create tracks where it would naturally disturb the loose stones. The gravel was then left to dry and any loose particles shaken off the board. Unfortunately, these tiny particles do have a tendency to get everywhere and you will probably need to go over the board with a soft brush to remove them all.

To complete the baseboard I needed to create the grassed areas. Before 'laying the turf' I made a soil sub-base by mixing together diluted PVA glue, Vallejo Brown Violet paint and *Celluclay*. This mixture was trowelled into place and left to dry, the edgings once again creating natural barriers to work up to. This was left to dry for forty-eight hours before applying the grass. The 'soil' was coated with PVA glue before sprinkling over static grass with my *Noch Gras-Master*. Unfortunately I think I was holding it a little too close to the board to try and prevent too much overspill and the grass came out a little too quickly. The excess was removed but some of the grass ended up a little flatter than hoped. As with the gravel, the static grass does get everywhere and will need cleaning up – however, it does not look unrealistic for a little stray grass to end up in the gravel, whereas stray gravel will look more out of place in the grass, and that's why I laid the finishes in this order.

Looking out at my own front lawn and path I realised that, with the best will in the world, there were still going to be some natural wild cards and so decided to add some stray long grass and a few buttercups and daisies. For the long grass I tore small pieces off a *Noch* grass mat and glued them in place, mainly at the edges of the grassed areas with some up against the concrete plinth to the launch platform. These were a little on the long side, so when the glue had dried I gave the tufts a haircut with a pair of nail scissors. I used a dried flower product from *Noch* to create the buttercups and daisies: these come in small circular arrangements and are extremely fragile. After a little trial and error I found the best way of handling the flowers was to cut the arrangement into four quadrants which retained some of the central stem to hold a couple of the individual flowers together. This, I found, was the only way to have enough to pick up with the tweezers so that I could dip the bunch into a little PVA glue before fixing in place. Light breathing is essential during this process if you'd rather not have a freshly planted carpet.

The Spaceport needed to be fenced off from the road and this was simply achieved using some plastic 'I' sections with their tips cut off at forty-five degrees and some aluminium mesh glued between them. To glue the mesh I used a new type of superglue made by *Loctite* called *Ultra*. This is supposed to be more flexible than ordinary superglue, which, as I am sure you are aware, can be quite brittle and weak when a shear force is exerted on it. *Ultra* worked well, as the flexibility of the mesh made getting a rigid joint very difficult otherwise. This was then airbrushed Hooker's Green and glued in place.

To complete the scene I envisaged that the fence ringed boundary would be softened with planting and so decided to add a tree to the strip of grass. There are many ways of creating model trees, but in this instance I used some dried Sea Moss, a naturally occurring product available from Model Railway suppliers and www.barrule.com, a marvellous web site for the supply of scratchbuilding and diorama materials. The dried Sea Moss does look remarkably like a naturally grown tree in miniature, but its trunk was a little too yellow in colour, so I gently airbrushed it at low air pressure using a mixture of Raw Umber and Neutral Grey. The Sea Moss is very fragile and must be handled with care if branches are not to break off. Because of the fragility issue I was concerned about what glue to use to affix the foliage, as trying to brush on PVA would surely cause the Sea Moss to break up. I got around this by spraying the future tree with *3M Photo Mount*, a spray-on glue used for sticking paper or photos to backing boards. Whilst spraying the glue I held the 'trunk' in my hand to create a natural mask before dipping the tree into a re-sealable plastic food bag containing some fine foam foliage from the same supplier as the Sea Moss. After a gentle shake the outer 'branches' were nicely foliated and the tree was glued into place after making a small hole in the baseboard to receive it. A very small sprinkle of *Woodland Scenics Earth Scatter* and dried herbs was glued around the base of the tree.

To finish off the base I glued the launch platform in position and applied some earth coloured *Mig Pigments* to the paving and gravel where dirt was likely to collect and to help break up the monotone colour of the gravel.

I gave the diorama a trial run by positioning the completed vehicles and realised that the section of cobbled road looked a little 'dead', so I added a further road vehicle pulling away from the Spaceport. A *Tamiya British Small Utility Vehicle* fit the bill nicely and this was constructed straight from the box with the painting completed before most of the construction. I used the same techniques for painting as discussed earlier and so won't repeat myself here. I then placed all the vehicles in their final position and glued all the figures in place. I had used superglue to fix the figures to *Games Workshop* figure bases to give me something to hold onto whilst painting them. This also enabled me to test-place all the figures, and have them standing, before deciding on a final arrangement.

My alternative history 'snapshot' was complete – *Dan Dare's Dad* is about to climb into a new rocket fighter and blast off on a mission he won't be returning from. It's being so cheerful that keeps me going.

In Reflective Mood

Placing a 1/5th scale Batman figure

in a shadowy Batcave lair

think the reason for *Batman*'s enduring appeal over the last seventy years is the fact that the character can be constantly re-interpreted, yet still remain *Batman*. During his lifetime he has been masked vigilante; intergalactic super-policeman; camp TV star; Dark Knight Detective; psychotic pensioner and everything in-between. My personal favourite versions of the *Caped Crusader* would have to be Denny O'Neil's and Neal Adams' interpretation of the early 1970s and Steve Englehart's and Marshall Rogers' version from the late '70s – early '80s. In my opinion, the best on-screen version has to be the early 1990s animated television series: Bruce Timm and Paul Dini managed to successfully distil the essence of what *Batman* is, yet still bring their own vision to each twenty-five minute episode.

Speaking of interpretation, *Dark Carnival Models* have put their own spin on the subject matter, albeit influenced by the artwork of Alex Ross, in a 1:5 resin model kit that expands and interprets two-dimensional imagery into the third dimension. Using the kit as a starting point I wanted to further expand that vision to create a diorama set in the *Batcave*.

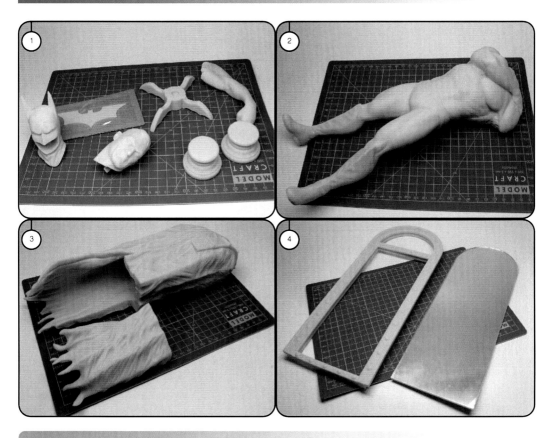

1-4: the kit's various component parts. Inset: test layout. 5: base is marked out with component positions. 6: cape joint.
7: after filling with superglue. 8: the join ground down. 9: after grinding is completed. 10: once cape is primed flaws become
visible. 11: putty applied to flaws. 12: *Batman* figure is primed and filled.

The kit comes as nine pieces cast in a 'porcelain'-type resin, which build into a standing figure plus his cape on a stand and a mirror. Also supplied is a cut section of mirror for the resin frame, but I would need to provide some brass tubing to complete the cape stand. This particular type of resin is very dense and can therefore sometimes be difficult to work, but fortunately the model is supplied with the worst of the seam-lines already removed, so all I needed to do was begin a course of weight training so that I could hold the figure for extended periods of time.

Before carrying out any preparatory work on the kit parts I gave some thought to the size of base I would need. I wanted this to be

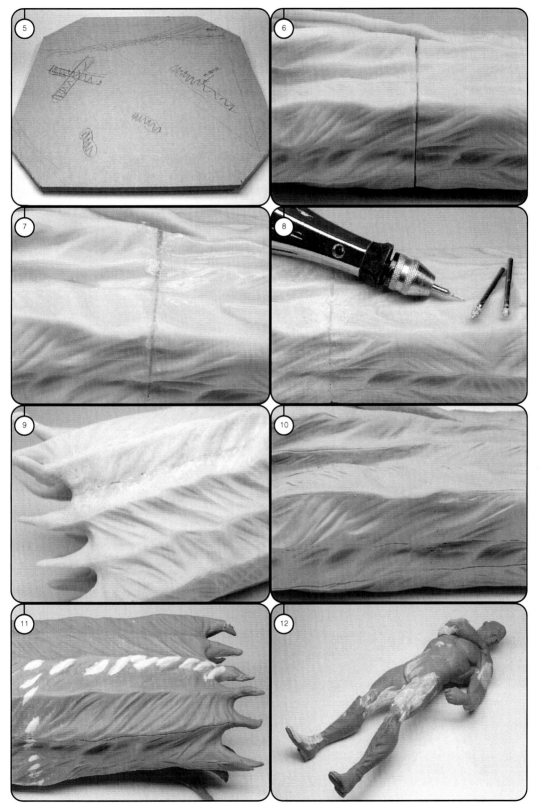

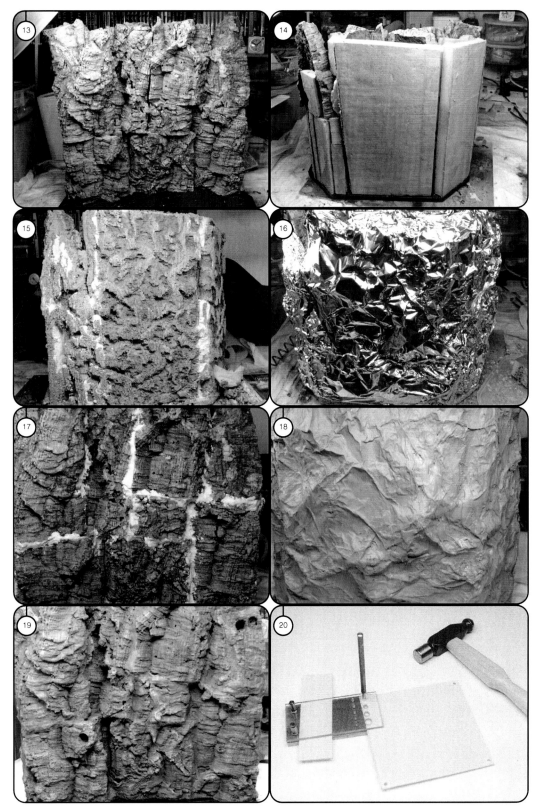

non-linear, as the pose of the figure does not lend itself to a specific front and back, which led to me considering a circular base. The largest circular cutting board I could find had a diameter of 320mm, which contained the kit parts nicely but left little room to expand the scene. I quite like using cutting boards as bases as they are pre-cut, pre-finished and robust. However, they do limit you to what is commercially available in your local home furnishings shop and so, if I want a large or unusually shaped base, I usually turn to 5mm *foamboard* or dense polystyrene. Unfortunately in this case the weight of the kit parts alone ruled out the use of these materials, meaning I had to resort to buying a sheet of 12mm thick *MDF* and cutting this to size.

When I say resort, I do mean *last* resort. I am not fond of cutting large boards, as things usually do not go to plan. After carrying a 1200 x 600mm sheet of *MDF* home on the tram and getting strange looks, which, truth be told, were less strange than the those I invited the day after when I had a 2m length of 15mm copper pipe tucked under my arm (more on that later), I decided to go for a base with the overall dimensions of 440 x 440mm. There are two very good reasons why I went for the 440mm measurement: firstly, a good base design allows for sufficient space around the figures without there being any 'dead space' between the different elements. The second reason is a little more prosaic: the only place I could find to store the model, and which would take the weight, was the top of a chest of drawers, which just happened to be 440mm wide.

As there was no way I was going to be able to cut out a neat circle in *MDF* I decided to go for the next best thing – an unequal octagon. After marking out the desired shape on the board it was time to cut it out. Now I have to admit that I don't like handling big tools (Stop sniggering at the back.). Perhaps it's due to lack of experience of handling big tools (What did I say about sniggering?) or the fact that I've never had any formal training in their use. I began by using a hand saw but have to admit that I quickly ran out of patience for this, deciding instead to get out my electric jigsaw. Let's just say that, whilst the baseboard was now cut out, the long edges weren't going to win any prizes for straight lines. I trimmed the board with 12mm plastic angles that, as well as straightening the edges, covered the cut edges of the *MDF* board that soak up paint like a sponge.

With the base board cut out I turned my attention to the kit parts, which, for the most part, fitted together superbly. Unfortunately the junction of the two cape parts was not a happy one, which I can quite imagine is due to the inherent difficulties of casting such large pieces of resin. To help the join I sanded away some of the material which gave the two parts a much closer match. I would just make the point that, when working with this type of resin you would be well advised to use a miniature power tool (insert your own joke here about the author's experience with large and small tools), otherwise it will take a long time and involve a lot of effort to work the resin manually. When I was satisfied that I had obtained

13-14: front and rear views of cork batcave wall. 15: carved rear face. 16: foil texture applied.

17: cork front face is filled. 8: gesso applied to foil. 19: front wall painted and holes created for dressing with plumbing.

20: holes punched in floor panels.

the best join possible, I drilled holes in the two parts so that I could insert some locating pins that would strengthen the joint. The parts were then glued together using a two-part epoxy glue, in this case *Araldite*. For dealing with relatively small parts such as these I use the quick drying version of *Araldite* as it gives you enough time to apply the glue to the parts without having to hold them together for an age whilst it sets.

Whilst the cape was setting I glued together the remaining parts, again with *Araldite*, as the weight of the pieces meant that superglue would not provide a sufficiently strong joint. Locating lugs and holes had been cast in the parts to help strengthen the joints and they mated together very well.

The two parts of the cape were securely glued together but there was a significant gap between them. To further strengthen the join and fill this gap I applied gel-type superglue with a toothpick to ensure that it was pushed well into the gap and quickly cured it with superglue accelerator. This gave me a very solid join that could then be worked with a grinding bit in my power tool. I actually used three different shapes of bit to allow me to work the join and surrounding resin and ensure that the seam line in the cape was continuous. I then gave the cape a coat of grey primer so that I could see the results of my work and check for any other imperfections. Whilst primer tends to come in grey, white and black, I find that the grey is best for highlighting any problems. On inspection I noticed that, during the grinding work, I had lost some of the folds in the cape and so used some two-part epoxy putty to recreate them. Using *Aves'* putty I mixed together the two component parts then rolled the mix into sausage shapes. I cut these to length and laid them in the appropriate place. Using a combination of metal dental tools and neoprene clay-shapers I then worked the epoxy putty into shape and smoothed it out with tap water. Using this method I worked along the join to try and make the junction imperceptible. When the putty was dry, and to better observe the results, I applied a further coat of grey primer. Holding the cape at different angles under the lamp I was mostly happy with the results but noticed that a little more work was needed to complete the cape satisfactorily. I therefore repeated the process.

Very little putty was required to hide the join between the body and head, and the body and left arm, but, on close inspection, I noticed some slight flaws that needed attention – a few rough grinding marks from the manufacturer's clean of the parts plus a few minor surface imperfections. To fill these I used two-part epoxy putty as described above, along with a couple of different materials to deal with the different types of imperfection. To fill the minor surface imperfections I applied *Squadron Green Putty* with an old scalpel blade. This was then smoothed out using acetone-based nail polish remover applied with cotton buds. To fill the grind marks I used *Vallejo's* fine surface filler, which was wiped on and off using a fingertip. The figure was then sanded down using increasingly finer grades of wet

21-22: floor laid and painted. 23: fan components. 24: grinding bits used to reduce wheel. 25: plumbing accessories.

26: pipes are painted and dirtied down. 27-28: base flesh coat applied to *Batman*.

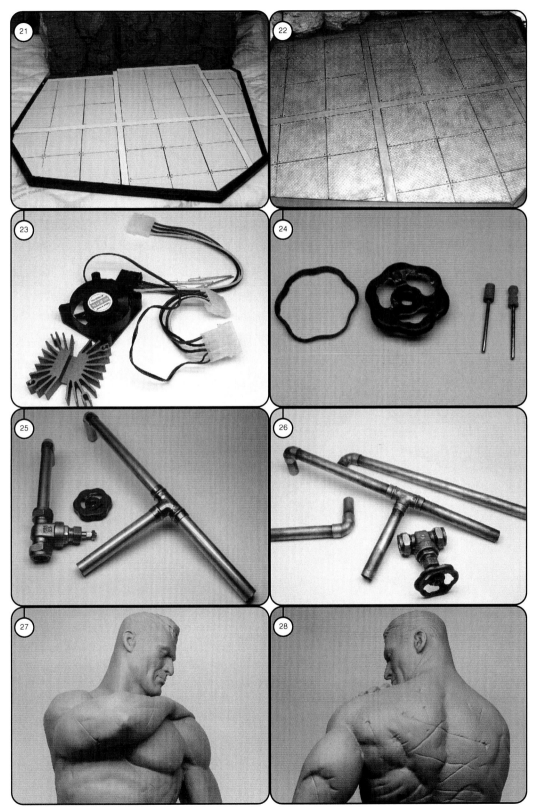

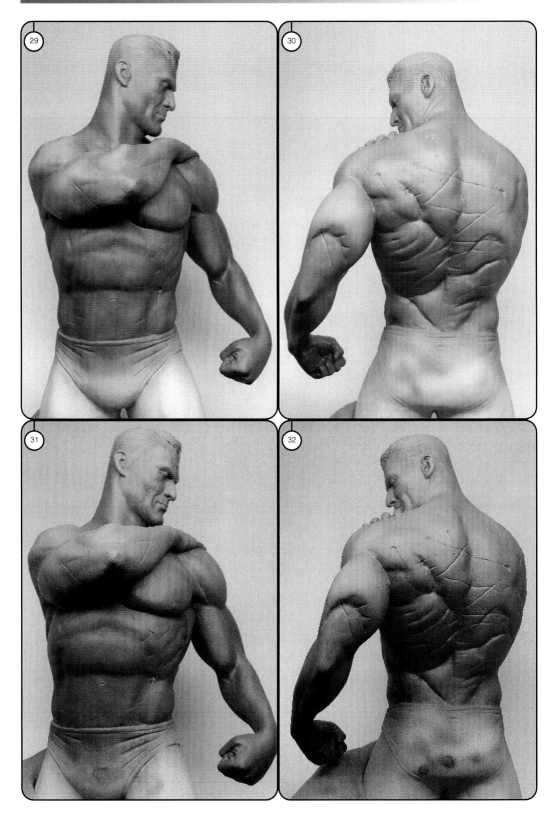

aluminium oxide paper to give a silky smooth finish. In some ways I may have gone over the top in finishing the figure off, but I have found that nothing highlights poor preparation more than bare flesh. All the sub-assemblies were given a coat of grey primer, except for the body that was based with white primer as it is easier to spray over light colours such as flesh, and, I believe, makes the flesh tones more vibrant than a dull undercoat.

It was now time to mix up some paint before firing up the airbrush. I mixed my standard flesh tone from approximately equal quantities of Raw Sienna, Burnt Sienna and Titanium White. This is probably a little on the dark side for a lot of skin tones, particularly if you stalk the streets of *Gotham City* by night (or live in Manchester), but it is a good starting point from which to mix the various flesh tones you will need. If you want a healthy, bronzed, tan look I would darken the colour using Burnt Sienna and Burnt Umber, which is a chocolate brown, but, in this instance, I wanted the skin tones to be slightly more subdued, so used Burnt Sienna and Raw Umber, which is a green brown, to create the darker shades. To lighten the base flesh tone I added Raw Sienna and Unbleached Titanium White in increasing quantities with some additional Titanium White added to the final highlight. Sometimes it is difficult to judge colours when mixing paints as they tend to dry a little darker than in their wet state. However, reviewing the lighter shades, I was concerned that the colour was looking a little on the yellow side, so I added a little Portrait Pink to the mixes to bring a touch of redness to them.

I used Neutral Grey for the tights, darkening them with Mars Black and lightening them with the addition of Titanium White. For the cape, boots and pants I decided to use an approximately 50-50 mix of Payne's Grey and Navy as the base colour, with pure Payne's Grey and Navy for the shade and highlight colours respectively.

With the paint mixed I went about airbrushing the flesh tones. I started by giving the figure an overall coat of my base flesh colour. I did this because the *Liquitex Soft Body Acrylics* I use are slightly more translucent than a lot of model specific paints, so having a solid base colour to work from means that I do not have to apply the shades in quite such thick layers to produce the desired tones. With the base colour down I then worked from dark to light, starting in the natural body recesses, and in this instance wounds, and finishing with the high points of the prominent muscles. This was then allowed to dry before the application of a coat of matt varnish to protect the work I had completed to this point.

The flesh areas were then masked off using *Tamiya* tape and kitchen towels to cover the bulk areas, and I sprayed the three tones of Neutral Grey onto the legs. Because of the complex curves around the groin and buttocks and at the junction with the boots I used *Blu-Tac* as a masking agent, with the remainder of the legs being protected with tape. I gave the pants and boots two coats of Paynes Grey, which is a most useful colour, being a very

29-30: shadows are airbrushed. 31-32: shadows are blended with base colour.

dark blue that, with enough coverage, becomes almost black. Add lighter colours to it, however, and the blue element in it comes back to life. These areas were then given a single highlight coat.

Whilst I was working with the airbrush I decided to paint the cape, which was first given a coat of Raw Sienna to act as a base for the yellow belt hung over its shoulder. I used Yellow Oxide as the base colour for the belt as I did not want it to be a bright yellow in finish. The belt was masked off with *Blu-Tac* and I gave the cape the two coats of Payne's Grey I had used for the pants and boots. I sprayed the highlight colour around the mask areas but decided that, because of the amount of creases and folds in the cape, I would be better off drybrushing any further highlights. The inside of the cape was treated to a further highlight of pure Navy as I wanted it to be like a traditional opera cape with a black outer and coloured inner lining. I drybrushed some Raw Umber and Neutral Grey to the base of the cape as I felt that, due to its length, it would more likely than not trail on the ground, picking up dirt. This was later repeated on the boots.

To save having to rest the cape on its back I chose to complete the cape stand by sponge-applying *Games Workshop's* Boltgun Metal and Chainmail to give the appearance of worn steel. I applied a little Raw Umber to the base to add further wear.

The figure now needed completing using washes to bring out the detail. Normally I would simply use thinned versions of my main flesh colours with, perhaps, some additional Raw and Burnt Umber. This figure is covered in bruises and scars, however, so I needed to create further colour variation by adding Yellow Oxide and Dioxazine Purple to the mixes. The scars were applied using *Games Workshop's* Scab Red, which is ideal for dry blood, rather than the usual *Hammer House of Horror* Tomato Ketchup Red. The washes were worked into the obvious battle-damaged areas and into the rib cage to imply that they were badly bruised. To avoid any hard edges to the washes I used cotton buds and my finger tip to smudge the edges.

The hair was painted black, but, rather than giving the edge of the hair a smooth line, I used the brush at ninety degrees to the hairline to try and give the impression of individual hairs, repeating this technique for the eyebrows. Black hair is very difficult to highlight with paints as, if you're not careful, it will end up looking grey. I mixed up an almost black-brown from Payne's Grey and Burnt Umber and drybrushed it across the head as a first highlight. I then added a little Neutral Grey to the mix and drybrushed it across the obvious highlighted areas.

To finish off my flesh painting I like to use pastel powders to add further shadowing and help blend the colours. I ground up some pastels on a sheet of sandpaper selecting colours similar to those I had used to mix my paint flesh tones. These powders can then be mixed

33-34: first highlights are added. 35-36: second layer of highlights are created.

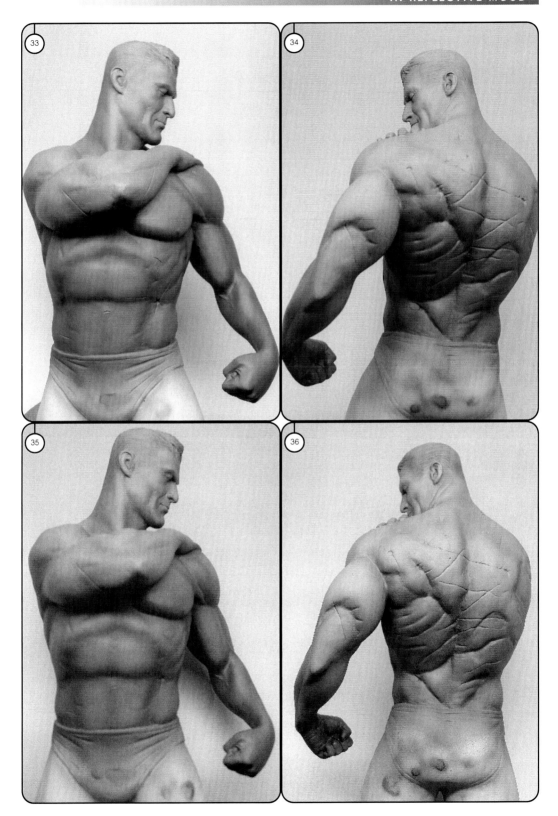

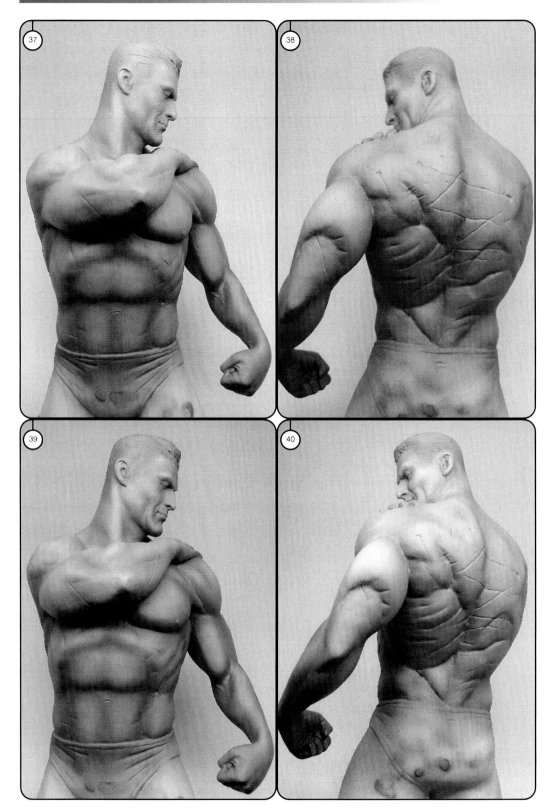

using an old brush to create the desired flesh tones and applied to the model with a chisel edge brush, which I find is good for working powder into the various nooks and crannies. The pastels were also most helpful in blending and accentuating the various wounds and bruises. I mixed together some Grey and Raw Umber coloured pastels to give *Bruce* a five-o'clock shadow and to also apply to the base of his rather severe haircut. Once satisfied with the application of the pastel powders I gave the whole thing a coat of matt varnish to seal the work to date.

Taking a break from the figure I returned to the base and gave some consideration to the construction of the rock face. I chose to use cork bark to replicate the look of rock, which is an old standby of Railway Modellers and can be easily picked up in hobby shops. However, buying a piece of cork bark in the size and shape I wanted was a non-starter, so I went about arranging smaller pieces to form the desired shape, gluing them together using a hot glue gun. The pieces needed had to be carefully positioned to minimise the gaps between them, although these could be dealt with later. I was very concerned about the stability of the cork if left on its own and decided to create a back wall to provide additional stability for the structure and finish off the rear of the model.

To create the rear wall I glued sections of 25mm thick insulation board to the base and each other and then partially filled the void with some off-cuts of the board. I then filled the void with lightweight *Hydrocal Plaster* to provide a solid backing to the front and rear walls – the board off-cuts help reduce the amount of plaster you will need and also keep the weight down. To ensure that the plaster did not leak out I filled all the gaps between insulation boards and cork bark with *Woodland Scenics Foam Putty*, a lightweight putty than can be carved when dry.

Whilst I could have simply sanded the rear face smooth and painted it black, I believe that a diorama should be able to be viewed 'in the round'. Admittedly, most dioramas will have a 'front' or an optimal viewing position, but this doesn't mean that the 'back' should be neglected. I therefore made up my mind to try and create a rock face for the rear of the wall without resorting to the use of more cork bark for two reasons: firstly, I am always keen to try different techniques, and, secondly, I was attempting to keep an eye on the budget for the project and, after paying over £25 for the bark for the front of the wall, I did not feel that the rear warranted such expenditure.

OK, its confession time. The rear wall did not turn out quite as originally envisaged. After successfully carving the insulation board previously to create a coursed stone wall I thought I would attempt to carve the rear wall in a similar way to create a rock effect. I therefore got out my riffling files and set to work carving out some rock faces, impressing texture into them using an off-cut of bark then sealing everything with a paste made from *Gesso* and very fine gravel. When I had finished I stepped back to admire my handiwork and

37-38: a third set of highlights is created. 39-40: the final set of highlights is added.

what should have been a rock wall looked more like crazy paving with an *Artex* coating... and if you think I'm printing a picture of that you can think again. Analysing the problem I realised that the *foamboard* was just too two-dimensional and so decided to attack it with a chisel blade to try and create a more three-dimensional feel. After having a good laugh at the results of this, I felt that I had made a right pig's ear of things and went away to sulk. Sorry – what I meant to say was, *after analysing the results of my explorations in 3D, I retired to contemplate a more successful approach to this ponderous situation.* However I describe it, I realised that everything I had done to date was simply too flat and regular and that I would need to try a different technique. Thinking of how set designers create rock faces I was reminded of the sets from the original series of **Star Trek** and laughed to myself at how most of them looked like wrinkled aluminium foil with a coat of emulsion paint – those that didn't look like polystyrene, anyway. *Bingo!* I had my answer and I raided the kitchen shelves for some foil, which I crunched up to create mounds and stuck to the board with hot glue. I then went over these and the rest of the insulation board with sheets of foil glued to the board with hot glue again. Safety note: hot glue is very hot and you will feel it through the foil. Who says I don't suffer for my art?

I realised that the foil would need some form of coating to strengthen it and provide a base for painting on. I was just about to apply my old faithful *Gesso* when I discovered that the bottle was empty. Taking a trip to my local Arts and Crafts shop to pick up more I found that *Liquitex* produce an *Extra Heavy Gesso* – at last, an art material named after me! I mixed this with some *Black Gesso* to create a grey colour for the base coat and went about brushing it onto the foil. Now, I must tell you that this stuff is thick. Really thick. If you think that the first time you made gravy using gravy granules and put too many granules in the liquid so that you could cut the gravy with a knife was thick, that is nothing compared to this *Gesso*. Having said that, the thickness of the *Gesso* worked to my advantage as the brush strokes created additional texturing. The work is slow and laborious as the *Gesso* can only be applied slowly because it needs to be worked into the foil, but with a gentle hand so that the foil is not damaged. The cork was given a coat of normal *Gesso* so that it could be worked into all the nooks and crannies, and in this instance I did not want to obscure, or add to, the existing texture.

When first considering the diorama I theorised that a habitable space underground would have some exposed pipework for both ventilation and plumbing purposes, and that's why I ended up bringing home a 2m length of copper pipe. Whilst plastic pipework would have been easier to work with the available diameter would have been both out of scale for the model and too intrusive on the diorama. Fortunately the copper pipe was fairly straightforward to cut to size with a cutting disc in my power tool and the fittings could be just push-fitted, or fixed with a little superglue – although I wouldn't suggest this if you're about to do some plumbing DIY at home. I used 90-degree bends to return the pipework

41: figure's flesh areas are masked off. 42: base grey added to leggings. 43-44: shadows are added and then blended with base colour. 45: highlights are created. 46: leggings masked. 47-48: a base coat of Payne's Grey is applied to boots followed by highlights.

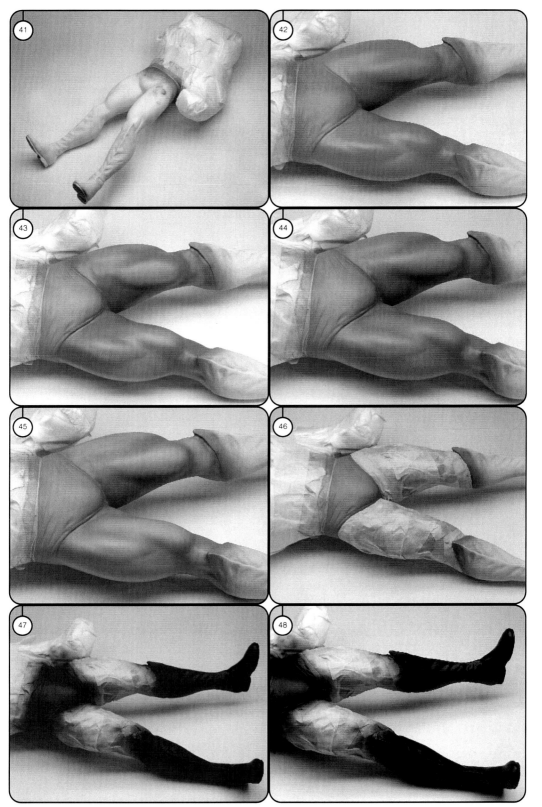

into the wall and a tee section to create a horizontal run. I chose to include a valve to add a little more visual interest and, whilst the wheel was of a suitable size to work at this scale, its thickness and spoke width were too great to be realistic. To rectify this I got out the cutting disc and started to thin the wheel. A further word of caution here – both the item you are cutting and your power tool are likely to get very hot, so I suggest holding the wheel with a thick cloth or an oven glove (but, for goodness sake, wash it before getting your tea out of the oven with it). It also helps to take short breaks whilst doing something like this as I have found that happiness is a cool tool (Is that worth trade-marking for a T-shirt slogan?). Using grinding bits I reduced the width of the spokes, taking the same precautions into account. The copper was then cleaned and primed for painting and given a spray coat of Aluminium from a rattle can. I cut holes into the cork bark to accept the pipework using a 16mm drill bit although, due to the softness of the wood, I was able to turn the bit by hand rather than getting out my electric drill.

Reviewing the paint finish to the pipe work the Aluminium looked too bright and unrealistic. To dull it down I applied some Boltgun Metal with a sponge, whilst leaving some of the Aluminium peaking through in random places. This gave the pipes an appearance closer to galvanised steel, but I felt it still needed a little more weathering and drybrushed the surface, particularly at joints and bends where grime would naturally accumulate. To finish off the weathering I brushed on and wiped off some *Liquitex Charcoal Woodstain* at each of the joints.

Turning my attention to the floor I had decided that, even if *Bruce* was working from the base of a cavern, the floor would be very uneven and he would have installed a level platform to work from. I chose to go with the industrial aesthetic and have the flooring representing metal tread plate panels with ducting for services between. I was fortunate enough to find some suitably textured *plasticard* on the Internet and cut it into 60mm square panels. In reality the panels would probably be larger but I liked the appearance I was getting with the small grids. To add a little more realism the floor panels would need to be fixed in place and so, using a punch and die set, I went about creating small holes in the corners of each of the panels. The duct covers between the panels were created from strips of plain *plasticard* and everything was fixed in place with PVA glue.

Going back to the practicalities of how you would use a space like this I added a wall-mounted ventilation unit, which I created using an old fan from a computer. For the fixings to the wall I used pop-rivets, which had sufficient length for fixing to an uneven wall and, again, are quite visually interesting. Once assembled, the fan unit was given a coat of black paint, the cabling being masked off with kitchen towel. The fan was then gently drybrushed with Boltgun Metal, Raw Sienna and Raw Umber to indicate wear and tear.

I wanted to take a break from the base and started to tackle the paintwork on the mirror. When modelling a large project, whilst it is not necessarily the most efficient way to proceed, it sometimes helps to change the focus of your attention so that you do not become too bogged down working on one thing. The mirror already has some wood grain texture to it and I decided I would add to this with the paint finish. Putting aside the airbrush for a

49: woodgrain effect created using transparent paint. 50: Tin Bitz sponge-applied to *Bat* symbol.

51: *Bat* symbol is finished off by sponging brass finish.

while I used a flat brush to apply a coat of Raw Sienna paint. Because we are trying to replicate the appearance of wood grain, in this instance it is actually desirable to leave your brush strokes visible – just try and keep them irregular and in the same direction, following the grain of the wood. If in doubt run your brush strokes along the length of the wood, which means that, for a framed item like the mirror, the brush strokes will run in different directions depending on whether you are painting a horizontal or a vertical member. And remember, you don't have to worry about totally even paint coverage, as this is just the undercoat for additional coats of paint. To further add to the grain I transferred to transparent paints at this point. Whilst shades of brown can be mixed using *Tamiya*'s Clear Green and Red, I prefer to use the range of transparent brown colours produced by *Liquitex*. I wanted the mirror to be a quite a dark timber colour but also wanted to add a little warmth to the colouring as most of the colour scheme for this project is based around cool blues and greys. Rather than simply applying a single coat of Transparent Burnt Umber I used a two-coat colour scheme that would add to the depth of the finish because I was using transparent paint. I started off by using Transparent Burnt Sienna and applying it using an old, flat brush – the older the better, as I wanted an uneven application with visible brush strokes. As with the base coat, the brush strokes are kept in the same direction as the grain of the wood.

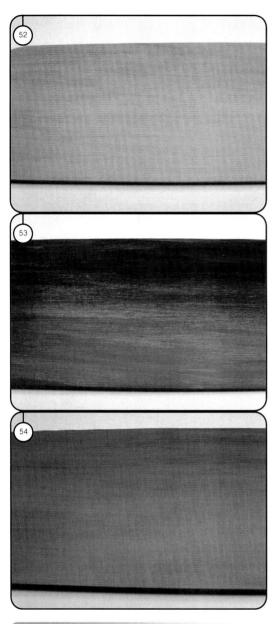

52: rear of mirror is painted in a natural wood finish.
53: woodgrain is applied. 54: grey wash is applied to age mirror.

When first applying the paint you may need to vary the direction of your brush strokes to get into all the tight corners – just brush it out in one direction once you've got the paint onto the model. After speeding up the drying time with a hair dryer I repeated the process using Transparent Raw Umber to darken the wood grain and give it a slightly more aged appearance. To finish the woodwork off I ran some *Liquitex Charcoal Woodstain* into the joints in the timber frame and lightly drybrushed some of the edges with Raw Sienna and Unbleached Titanium White to obtain a slightly worn effect.

The mirror is trimmed with circular mouldings and the kit is supplied with a bat symbol to finish it off. I had already decided that the mirror was an old item of furniture and so did not warrant any bright metal trim. I base-coated the mouldings with *Games Workshop Tin Bitz* and drybrushed them with Brass. I used the same colours on the bat symbol but applied them with a sponge on a black base coat to try and give the appearance of beaten, as well as old, metal. My justification of an old metal bat symbol comes from a 1950s' issue of the *Batman* comic which tells how *Thomas Wayne* dresses up in a bat costume for a fancy dress party, which in turn influences young *Bruce* when he decides on his own crime-fighting costume. I justified that the *Wayne* family fortune could extend to *Wayne* senior buying this mirror at the same time as the costume and having the bat symbol added to it as the whim of someone who has money to spare.

Because we are dealing with a scene in the round the rear of the mirror also had to be painted. It comes with a grey, textured rear, but I wanted to give it the appearance of worn plywood. I used the previously described techniques on the mirror, this time choosing *Vallejo* Natural Wood and Woodgrain. This was too fresh looking so I repeated the technique with a thick wash of *Liquitex* Neutral Grey. With the paint dry I glued it to the back of the frame using *PVA* glue, very aware that I would only get one go at this and even then I might suffer the squidge factor on the facing surface. Sure enough, when I had let the glue dry and picked up the mirror some of the *PVA* had seeped onto the reflective front. All was not lost, however, as, with a sharp new blade in my scalpel, I was able to carefully cut around the perimeter of the glue and gently prise it off the surface with no ill effect.

With the mirror complete I returned to the cave wall and, after some consideration, decided to use *Woodland Scenics Earth Pigment* colours to paint the rock. These are designed to be used as a wash on porous surfaces such as plaster, but can also be applied 'neat' to non-porous surfaces such as the foil I had used for the rear of the wall. By coating both faces of the wall with *Gesso* I knew I would get the same level of absorbency of the paints and, therefore, the same finish to the differing materials on both sides of the wall. Using Yellow Ochre, Raw Sienna, Stone Grey and Slate Grey I applied the paint randomly and, using the slow drying times of these paints to my

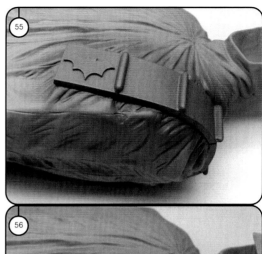

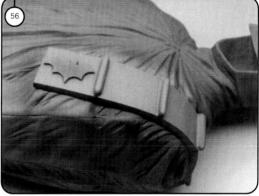

55: base coat of Raw Sienna is applied to the *Bat belt*.
56: Yellow Oxide highlights are then added.

advantage, I worked the colours into each other to blend them and get some – hopefully – natural tonal variations. I also worked some black wash into the deep recesses, but kept this to a minimum as I did not want to make the colours any darker than they already were. The wall was left to dry overnight before lightly drybrushing some Neutral Grey to pick up some of the textural variations. This was done sparingly over the foil rear as, even though the foil had been reinforced with the *Heavy Gesso*, it was still far from being a robust backing, and I was concerned that vigorous drybrushing could tear the material. I followed the drybrushing with a wash of Raw Umber to tone down some of the Neutral Grey and create further colour variation.

Once I was satisfied with the wall I turned my attention to the floor. I needed a black base coat for the metallic finish to the chequer plate panels and, rather than mask off the wall, I brush-applied a coat of black craft paint, thinning it so that it could be worked into the recesses between panels. Craft paint can sometimes be an economic alternative to artist's and model colours, particularly when covering large areas, especially if it is not going to be the final finish. I mixed up a base colour of *Games Workshop*'s Black and Boltgun Metal in an approximate 1:1 ratio and drybrushed this over the whole floor area, working it into all

57-58: various views of the completed *Batman* figure. Wounds are added to complete the look.

areas but not overly worrying about getting a completely even finish. When working on a large area like this I use a medium sized make-up brush, as these are ideal for drybrushing and are relatively cheap to replace – just don't use them to put on your eye shadow after painting with them. I then gave the panels a further drybrush with pure Boltgun Metal to pick up the raised detailing. Because these panels have a lot of raised detailing they would, in real life, pick up a considerable amount of grime and dirt, be very difficult to clean, and, depending on the cave's particular environmental conditions, could be subject to some oxidation. To replicate this weathering I gave the panels a drybrush with Raw Sienna and a wash of Raw Umber. I dried the paint off using a hair dryer and then went

59

60

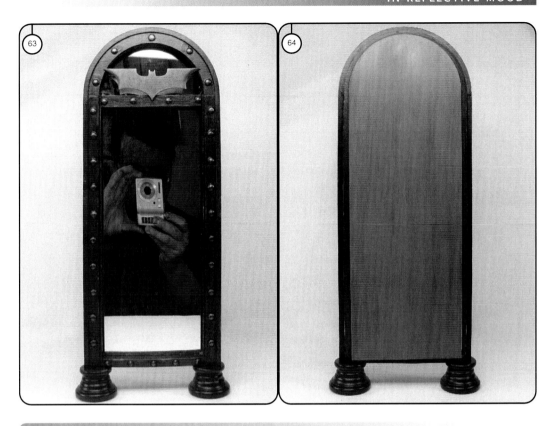

61-62: front and rear views of cape on stand. Notice base of stand carries through the *Bat* motif. 63-64: the completed mirror. 65: the completed floor prior to adding brass pegs to accept the figure and furniture. Fan and plumbing in place.

66: the rear wall is finished. 67: brass pegs are used to locate the *Batman* figure, cape stand and mirror.

back with a light drybrush of Boltgun Metal as the raised sections of the panels would be subject to wear that would rub off some of the collected detritus. I then used a black wash to run between the panels.

Looking at the completed wall and floor I was left with a hard edge between them, which would naturally disappear in shadow. To blur the edges between the two I got out some black *Mig Pigment* Powder and applied it to the junction of the two materials. Normally I would fix any pigment powder with a coat of varnish, but I did not want to change the finish of the floor. I therefore chose to leave the powder 'loose' as it would rarely be touched in the location it was in. To finish off the base I brush-applied some black paint to the edge angle trim. Mind you, when I say 'finish off', I still had to fit the vent pipes and fan unit. Fortunately, my hole drilling had been accurate enough that all the pipework push-fitted together and into the cork wall. A little bit of the floor finish was scratched as I pushed the pipe in place, but this was soon touched up with a little drybrushed Boltgun Metal. Some black *Pigment* Powder was brushed around where the pipes join the floor and I then applied Rubble Dust *Pigment* Powder to the horizontal surfaces of the fan and pipes to indicate the inevitable accumulation of dust that appears in a single man's place of abode.

It was now time to bring all the elements together, but I was very concerned about the total weight of the completed model if all the components were glued to the base, which, on its own, was a fair old weight. Because the components were fairly well balanced on their own and all of a good weight I realised that I did not have to worry too much about them falling over without glue to hold them in place, but I did want a means of securely locating them onto the base. To this end I drilled holes in the underside of each component and reciprocal holes in the base, into which I glued sections of brass rod that the parts could then merely sit on to stay where they should.

With the model complete my chest of drawers was the proud accommodator of a section of the *Batcave* – just don't ask me to make room for the *Batmobile* or the *Giant Penny*, please.

HOBBY MATERIALS INDEX

Airfix
http://www.airfix.com/

Aves Studio
http://www.avesstudio.com/

Bachman
http://www.bachmanntrains.com/   http://www.bachmann.co.uk/

Bandai
http://www.bandai.com/

Barrule – Antenociti's Workshop
http://www.barrule.com/

Celluclay
http://www.activaproducts.com/

Dapol
http://www.dapol.co.uk/

Faller
http://www.faller.de/

Games Workshop
http://www.games-workshop.com/

Lifecolor
http://www.lifecolor.com/

Liquitex
http://www.liquitex.com/

Mayfair Games
http://www.mayfairgames.com/

Microscale Industries
http://www.microscale.com/

MIG Productions
http://www.migproductions.com/

Milliput
http://www.milliput.com/

MiniArt models
http://miniart-models.com/

Noch
http://www.noch.de/de/   http://www.noch.de/en/

Pegasus Hobbies
http://www.pegasushobbies.com/

Plastruct
http://www.plastruct.com/

Plus Models
http://www.plusmodel.cz/

Revell
http://www.revell.com/

Schleich's
http://www.schleich-s.com/

Swann Morton
http://www.swann-morton.com/

Squadron
http://www.squadron.com/

Tamiya
http://www.tamiya.com/

Vallejo
http://www.acrylicosvallejo.com/

Woodland Scenics
http://www.woodlandscenics.co.uk/   http://www.ecscenics.co.uk/

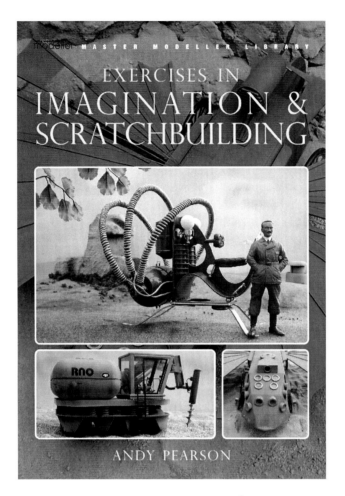

... and for even more
of what you bought this volume for...

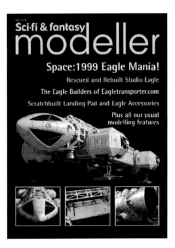

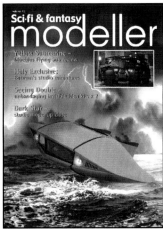

Sci.fi & fantasy modeller

published quarterly - 100 pages, all colour, softcover format.

£13.95 UK

Order online at: www.scififantasymodeller.co.uk

Barry Ford was born in 1966 in Bury, Lancashire, UK and has never strayed very far from there. His earliest memories are of watching **Thunderbirds** on his mother's knee as a toddler.

The downhill slide into obsession started there.

From an early age Barry tried to make things and was always frustrated that his toilet roll holders and sticky-backed plastic never looked as good as John Noakes'. When not watching the works of Gerry Anderson or **Star Trek** as a child Barry could usually be found drawing or painting. Unless he was reading American comics, of course – another of his passions. With these influences it was only a matter of time before he gravitated towards the shelf of model kits at the local newsagent, particularly when he spotted the *Airfix Interceptor* from **Captain Scarlet** and the *Aurora Enterprise* kit.

Barry's parents encouraged his creative endeavours and, when the limited number of SF kits available at the time ran out he began working through the *Airfix* kits most boys born in the 1960s and '70s will be familiar with.

Entering his teenage years modelling took a back seat until he came across *Bandai's* re-issues of Japanese **Thunderbirds** kits in the mid 1980s and began to take model making seriously.

Barry studied Architecture at Manchester University for three years before deciding to become an Architectural Technologist rather than a Design Architect. This slight change in career can be summed up in two instances: during one critique session the tutor likened his design to something out of **Fireball XL5**. Barry thought he was praising his work – but later found out he wasn't. In another review session a tutor commented that, whilst his design wasn't the prettiest in class, it was the only one that was structurally sound.

Architecture as a career is a natural progression of Barry's desire to create things – the big difference being that, during the day he works to a much larger scale than he does in his free time. He has worked for *Byrom Clark Roberts* in Manchester since 1988 and is currently an Associate there with a team of four working under him. In addition to his qualification as a Chartered Architectural Technologist he is also a Chartered Environmentalist; a Chartered member of the Institute of Building and a CDM Co-ordinator.

During the late '80s Barry discovered limited run 'garage' kits and his modelling focus from then on was purely science fiction and fantasy orientated due to the wide variety of subjects becoming available as models. He admits to becoming very anally retentive about model making at one stage – obsessing over every last detail and colour shade, but, after a few years of this, he began to realise he was getting older and the pile of kits on top of the wardrobe was not getting any smaller. If he did not stop fretting over things that didn't really matter he was never going to get anything built, and, most importantly, wasn't going to have any fun with what is supposed to be a relaxing hobby.

With this revelation Barry's modelling skills started to improve. He was no longer scared of trying new techniques, working on the principal that even if it didn't turn out right he would have learned something from it.

Many of Barry's modelling skills are self taught, but he has also picked up a great deal over the years by reading books and magazines, both subject-related and from other modelling genres, as he believes we can all learn something from each other.

As Barry has grown older the challenge has moved away from purely creating stand-alone models towards placing models into realistic environments, with the ultimate goal being to try and tell a story with his dioramas.

Barry currently lives with his dog, Honey. During the course of writing most of this book his faithful companion was Hattie, who passed away in the summer of 2009, aged 15.